Where's the Wonder in Elementary Math?

TRANSFORMING TEACHING

Series Editor: James Fraser, NYU Steinhardt School of Culture, Education, and Human Development

Routledge
Taylor & Francis Group
711 Third Avenue
New York, NY 10017

Routledge
Taylor & Francis Group
2 Park Square
Milton Park, Abingdon
Oxon OX14 4RN

© 2008 by Taylor & Francis Group, LLC
Routledge is an imprint of Taylor & Francis Group, an Informa business

International Standard Book Number-13: 978-0-415-95716-8 (Softcover) 978-0-415-95715-1 (Hardcover)

Library of Congress Cataloging-in-Publication Data

McVarish, Judith.
   Where's the wonder in elementary math? : Encouraging mathematical reasoning in the classroom / Judith McVarish.
      p. cm. -- (Transforming teaching)
   Includes bibliographical references and index.
   ISBN 978-0-415-95715-1 (hb) -- ISBN 978-0-415-95716-8 (pb) 1. Mathematics--Study and teaching (Elementary)--United States. 2. Mathematics--Study and teaching (Primary)--United States. I. Title.

QA135.6.M398 2007
372.7--dc22   2007008693

Visit the Taylor & Francis Web site at
http://www.taylorandfrancis.com

and the Routledge Web site at
http://www.routledge.com

Where's the Wonder in Elementary Math?

Encouraging Mathematical Reasoning in the Classroom

Judith McVarish

Routledge
Taylor & Francis Group
New York   London

To Mark, Nate, and Heather

For more reasons than there are pages in this book

Contents

Acknowledgments

I wish to thank many who contributed in multiple ways to this work: Anthony Bambrola, Carol Thibideau, Jae Goodwin, Rosemary Vickery, Amy Leicht, Meg Smanik, Tyson Schrader, Gordon Pradl, Laura Hopsfenberger, Rob Cohen, Elizabeth Quintero, Margot Ely, John Maynard, Mary Van Valin, Nathan McKelvey, John Anzul, and Belen Matias. I wish to express my gratitude in particular to each of the students, parents, and teachers of the *In Addition* After School Mathematics Initiative. My deepest appreciation to each of the students in classes that I now teach, have taught in the past, and will teach in the future as you keep my mind active and curious.

A very special thank you to my friend Margaret Anzul, for reading and rereading with a critical, caring, and curious eye.

Please share your thoughts and comments with me at mcvarishj@stjohns.edu

or, as the banner in the classroom McVarish describes proclaims, "All of us are wiser than any of us." And publications, like McVarish's work, are one key element in this essential dialogue and the achievement of this wisdom.

In this volume the voices of scholars and the leaders in the field who first launched the standards movement in mathematics are brought into a thoughtful dialogue with public school classroom teachers who have made their classrooms come alive with mathematical meaning and mathematical success. McVarish orchestrates this dialogue and invites the rest of us in. We are wiser for being her guests.

James W. Fraser

Professor
Steinhardt School of Culture,
Education, and Human Development
New York University

Chapter 1

Setting the Stage

The 28 fourth graders in Mrs. Thomas's class are congregated on a rug in front of the windows talking about the large graphic representation on the floor in front of them. The discussion is animated and filled with reasoning and speculative theories. No one is raising a hand to speak or waiting for a nod from the teacher. The dialogue moves from student to student with only the occasional question from the teacher. The students have spent the previous weeks surveying all 1,000 people in their school about the question, "Do you like school?"

Many discussions have already taken place and decisions made regarding how to collect, sort, and represent the data. Should the answer be provided verbally? Or would it be better to require a written response? Students even entertained the ideas of collecting the data in large group settings rather than surveying individuals or of using a collection box to gather the responses. Once the data have been collected, countless hours were spent working on how to categorize the responses. These categories included the students in grades K–6, their classroom teachers, the kitchen staff, the two custodians, the nurse, the principal and vice principal, the librarian, gym teachers, art and music teachers, and the resource room teachers and counselors, plus the three secretaries who work in the office.

Students gave reasons pro and con to support placing the classroom teacher responses with the data from their individual grades or into a category of their own. They also had to decide whether the office workers were considered administration or whether another category had to be created. If classroom teachers were included in the grade-level data, students then had to consider what to do with the data from special subject teachers. The next phase in the process was to determine how to visually display the results. Students experimented with several different graphing styles and concluded that a simple bar graph allowed readers to see the results most clearly. Yet this provided another dilemma of how to represent the data since a one-to-one representation would create bar lengths that were unmanageable. Students grappled for some time before arriving at a mathematical key of 5 people per inch for their graphic representation in order to accommodate the large number of responses in some categories.

Now, as students sat on the carpet in a semicircle, looking at their 8-foot by 4-foot finished graphic representation, discussion focused on the fact that all categories showed more YES responses than NO responses—except the third-grade category.

Susie: Who went in to the third grade to ask them?
Alisha and Brianna: We did.
Susie: Did you say, "WHO likes school?" (Susie demonstrates by speaking with a dreaded intonation) or did you say, "Who likes school?" (Again Susie demonstrates with a lilt at the end of the question as if asking who likes ice cream.)

Alisha and Brianna proceeded to demonstrate the neutrality of their voices during the visit to the third grade.

Susie: I think it is because it's not cool to like school in the third grade. I would have said "no" if someone asked me last year.
Jorge: Yeah, remember how we were afraid of not being cool?
Mrs. Thomas: Is there a way you might have prevented the cool factor in your questioning?
Tim: Have them write down their answer.
Kim: But they would still think we expected them to say NO. I think we should have given them a secret ballot kind of vote.
Max: Maybe it's not the third grade they don't like. I mean, it's only October, so it could be second grade they didn't like.
Susie: I don't think it was second grade though, 'cause little kids like school more.
Brianna: Well we know it's not the third-grade teachers they didn't like. They're awesome.
Alisha: Yeah, it's not the teachers. I went and asked Mrs. Blake what she thought, and she didn't think they've been in third grade long enough to not like it.
Mrs. Thomas: So, how could we find out for sure?

It is obvious these students have had many opportunities to exchange mathematical ideas because this discourse is free flowing. Students are building on the math thinking of their classmates—questioning each other and responding in a manner that is more collaborative than defensive or competitive. Collaborative dialogue such as this encourages students to think critically. The teacher's questions were not aimed at mathematics facts, such as "How many fewer third graders like school than fourth graders?" Rather they were targeted at getting students to think and solve problems. Thoughtful teacher questions elicit responses that require more than computational, procedural, lower-level math thinking.

When I walk into a classroom and see and hear children actively engaged in questioning each other and talking breathlessly about why they think something is so or not so, I ask myself, "How did this teacher create this kind of mathematics environment? Is this happenstance or is there something behind the scene that is important to understand?" Being involved in teaching and learning that foster discussion, debate, and the construction of mathematical ideas is appealing for students and teachers alike. It taps into the reason most of us went into teaching in the first place. Have you ever met a teacher who claimed his or her career choice was motivated by something other than making a difference, helping children to learn deeply in engrossing and exciting ways, and wanting students to engage in learning of any kind with joy? What happens to dismantle this vision? This book is about exploring ways to foster creativity and critical thinking in the classroom and how to make mathematics learning a joyful journey for all stakeholders. It is intended as a mathematics resource text for pre-service and in-service teachers of elementary school children who want to foster critical thinking and mathematics reasoning in their classrooms.

Young children begin their schooling journey filled with expectation, questions, vim, vigor, openness, and innocence. Where along this learning journey do students develop the stance of "playing school," the attitude of "doing what the teacher wants," or "how many minutes until recess?" Why has it become "cool" for students to say that they don't like school as they progress through the grades? Margaret Donaldson (1978) raises this question in *Children's Minds* when she speaks about large numbers of students leaving school feeling defeated and lacking any excitement in the pursuit of intelligence:

> In the first few years at school all appears to go very well. The children seem eager, lively, and happy. There is commonly an atmosphere of spontaneity in which they are encouraged to explore and discover and create. However, when we consider what has happened by the time children reach adolescence, we are forced to recognize that the promise of the early years frequently remains unfulfilled. (pp. 13–14)

Throughout this book I will investigate these questions and others and discover ways to fill the classroom culture with mathematics thinking opportunities for both students and teachers. These opportunities will be embedded in the questions that are asked, in the transitions between the activities of the day, and in the homework that is assigned. When the culture of the mathematics classroom shifts from one of compliance and right answers to an interest in the how and why of that which surrounds us, the energy level is raised and the engagement of students and teachers alike becomes heightened.

LEARNING AND TEACHING MATHEMATICS: A HISTORICAL PERSPECTIVE

Historically, mathematics was considered a discipline of right answers, formulas, and procedural rules. It was a male-dominated field of study and considered a discipline where only mathematically gifted students went on to higher levels of mathematical study. The mathematics content offered in elementary school remained primarily in the realm of number operations and functions with little attention given to geometry, data analysis, probability, and reasoning. The teacher stood at the blackboard and demonstrated for students the proper procedure to reach a correct solution. This was typically followed with practice problems for students to complete at their seats, without discourse with fellow classmates.

In the last 20 years, however, there has been a national standards movement in mathematics education that has important implications for both teachers and the students they teach. We are in the midst of a revolution in teaching and learning mathematics that was originally fueled by the publication *Curriculum and Evaluation Standards for School Mathematics* by the National Council of Teachers of Mathematics (NCTM, 1989). This council is the largest international professional organization in the field of mathematics education. The document suggested a new direction for mathematics teaching and learning and provided the pedagogy to deliver the suggested content and evaluation practices. Elementary school mathematics was no longer limited to the arithmetic of days gone by where students only learned to add, subtract, multiply, and divide. The newly published *Standards* called for expansion of the elementary mathematics curriculum to include data analysis, probability, patterns and functions, algebra, reasoning, geometry, and communicating mathematical ideas, both verbally and in writing. Although computation skills were addressed in the *Standards* document, a decrease in attention to rote memorization of facts and algorithms was advocated. Instead of rote computation and memorization, conceptual understanding, connections, and application were to be emphasized. This benchmark publication articulates a vision for mathematics teaching and learning that includes having *all* students value and become confident in their ability to do mathematics. An important goal is for *all* students to become mathematical problem solvers who learn to communicate and reason mathematically. The *Standards* offered guidelines designed to prepare students to be informed citizens in the world into which they would graduate.

These guidelines identified exploration, questioning, debate, reasoning, and communication as critical and necessary skills for all students.

In the same year, *Everybody Counts: A Report to the Nation on the Future of Mathematics Education* (NRC, 1989) was published. The National Research Council (NRC) was organized in 1916 to function as the operating agency of both the National Academy of Sciences and the National Academy of Engineering. The NRC is responsible for research in the field of mathematical sciences. *Everybody Counts* strongly advocated a need to alter the mathematics being taught in the schools, outlining how transitioning from an industrial society to an information society and a technology explosion have dramatically affected business, government, industry, and the home. The authors stated that mastery of mathematical facts and rules alone would no longer suffice to equip students to understand and participate in this ever-changing, technological world, where computation skills need to be coupled with conceptual understanding. The mathematics needed to be successful in the 21st-century workplace would require more mental analysis and communication of ideas and less perfunctory maneuvering of numbers. Technological expertise would be necessary for all (NRC, 1989).

Both the NCTM and the NRC provided the rationales for such a teaching and learning change. The protection of the environment, medical advances, space exploration, nuclear energy, inflation, and national debt were all given as examples of complex issues requiring an informed electorate who could interpret the world and make crucial, reasoned decisions and critically analyze data based on logic and mathematical reasoning (NRC, 1989). There are economic and societal issues that drive this reform, as well as educational demands. The demographics of our society are changing rapidly. One in every three American students is a member of a minority, and in the next decade minority populations will become the majority. Poverty, the need for instruction in English as a second language for our growing and diverse immigrant population, and stresses on family structures raise the stakes for all and underscore the need for true equity in all aspects of society. Mathematics teaching, which has traditionally discriminated against individuals on the basis of gender, class, and ethnicity, now must create "math equity" for all students. Advanced mathematics can no longer be reserved for white males, who now make up the overwhelming majority of those currently dominating the field of mathematics. Women and minorities must be given every opportunity to learn in order to enter fields involving mathematics and technology and to function effectively in the new global environment if we are to eliminate the elitist filter that currently exists and compromises students' potential to learn mathematics (NRC, 1989).

Again, in 1990, another seminal document by the NRC, *Reshaping School Mathematics: A Philosophy and Framework for Curriculum*, was published by the Mathematical Sciences Education Board (MSEB), which is governed by the National Research Council. The MSEB, yet another national organization, demanded a change from the instructional practices of 20, 50, or even 100 years ago in mathematics curricula and pedagogy. This document proposed a framework for national school mathematics reform that included improving the education of mathematics teachers through continuous professional development offerings to improve teacher efficacy and raise teachers' confidence in teaching mathematics, while encouraging alternative teaching methods. The thrust of this report was a drastic reform call for new materials and assessment methods to accompany suggested new content and pedagogy. The report also advocated that money be appropriated for new textbooks that embraced standards-based teaching and learning, as well as for materials such as mathematics manipulatives, computers, and calculators.

In April 2000, after 10 years of reflection and discussion among all constituents concerned with mathematics education, the NCTM published *Principles and Standards for School Mathematics: An Overview.* It revised, clarified, and refined the original document, while still maintaining the original vision set forth in 1989. The focus of mathematics learning in recent years has been on problem solving, including every aspect of mathematics education from creating problem-based curricula to including open-ended problems on standardized tests to posting problem-solving steps in classrooms.

Based on more than 30 years' experience as a teacher and teacher educator, I have been influenced by these documents, as well as by the works of Dewey (1938/1963) on constructivism and experiential learning, Vygotsky (1986) on the collaborative construction of understanding and his model of the zone of proximal development, Duckworth (1987) on "the having of wonderful ideas," Mezirow (1990, 1998) on self-regulation and transformative learning, and Freire (1970, 1973, 1996) on learning as liberation, social justice, and problem posing. The combination of these influences has convinced me that educators best help students understand their worlds by developing students' habits of wonder and wanting to know.

The Current Scene

School classrooms are situated at the epicenter of a series of expectations and obligations, each with its own set of controls and mandates. These expectations are manifested nationally on a large scale in such mandates as No Child Left Behind and NAEP testing. State controls are often financial or are directed at teacher accountability. Districtwide mandates may be curriculum based, union negotiated, or related to administrative policy. Schools have their own sets of expectations that come from parents, bus schedules, principals, and the culture of the teaching community. The cumulative effect of these expectations and outside influences can radically reduce the wonder and curiosity that are the cornerstones of learning engagement. So what options do teachers have as they try to meet all the demands placed on them and still create a learning environment that is filled with thinking and mathematics excitement? This book is about teaching in spite of all the mandates and control mechanisms and about helping teachers find more joy and less frustration in their teaching practice in spite of the layers of control influencing what and how they teach. Each chapter discusses ways teachers might infuse critical thinking opportunities into everyday teaching spaces in order to help children engage in mathematics learning that is more meaningful than test preparation instruction alone. It is indeed possible to meet the national, state, district, and school power forces and also bring teacher satisfaction and learning excitement into the classroom by incorporating small changes into peripheral teaching spaces.

This book is the result of my journey as a teacher and mathematics educator. I went from being a math student who was anxious and lacking confidence in my own abilities to becoming a teacher who studied strategies that would help students become confident solvers of problems. My goal is to support students in becoming capable of thinking, reasoning, and communicating in the process of solving problems successfully and with confidence and competence.

CONCEPTUAL CONVICTIONS

My own history with mathematics has led me to a series of mathematics conceptual convictions regarding the learning and teaching of mathematics that I adhere to strongly. It is this set of convictions that I believe helps me encounter mathematics with confidence and competence. In turn, I believe that if we nurture these conceptual convictions in the children we teach they, too, will engage in mathematics with capability and vigor. The convictions are:

A conviction that math is everywhere.

A conviction that everyone's voice counts.

A conviction that it takes persistence to solve mathematics problems.

A conviction that inquisitiveness is the beginning and end of problem solving.

A conviction that patterns help us to solve problems.

A conviction that learning is bigger than a test.

In addition, I believe these conceptual convictions promote students who are more likely to be learning goal learners than performance goal learners (Dweck, 2000). Carol Dweck differentiates between the two types of learners by describing performance goal learners as those who learn to "look smarter" in contrast to learning goal learners, who learn "to get smart."

The Convictions in Practice

Creating a cognitive climate that fosters the development of a series of conceptual convictions may in turn lead to increased engagement in the mathematics learning process and help to prepare students to become adaptive learners who can apply their understandings in new, unpredictable situations. The connection between developing positive mathematics convictions in children and successful mathematical thinking and reasoning is the increased level of engagement that takes place with the mathematics and the thinking around it. When learners' convictions are strong, they are more likely to connect their thinking to their own experience and to engage more cognitive resources in finding a solution. They will have more to say about the problem because it will be connected to more of their thinking. Below I describe these conceptual convictions that help students to become adaptive, engaged problem solvers and highlight the role of the teacher in developing these convictions in the children they teach.

A Conviction That Math Is Everywhere

We are surrounded by mathematical patterns and applications in the everydayness of our lives: which way we walk or commute to school, how many minutes until recess, how to pack the trunk of the car to fit everyone's suitcase, and how long it will take to save for a new pair of sneakers. It is the teacher's role to provide opportunities in classrooms and throughout the day that require observation, wonder, and time for children to make decisions on their own without constant direction from the teacher. In a third-grade classroom in East Harlem the idea for having turtle races came from a conversation a third-grade teacher had with a group of children one Monday during afternoon recess. Donny had received a new dog for his birthday, and this prompted a dialogue about pets. The teacher talked about her own pets with the children, starting with her cat that lives in Florida with her parents and ending with two miniature turtles named Fluffy and Feisty. One of the students asked if Feisty got his name because he was faster then Fluffy. The teacher asked the students how she would know which turtle was faster, and Jasmine, one of her students, suggested she race them. Tania shared with the group that she had turtles at home, and when they were put on the floor they would run away. This led to the suggestion of putting the two turtles in a controlled area to race each other. When asked what types of area might work for a race between two turtles, Rolf suggested putting them in a box, cutting a hole in it, and seeing who gets through the hole first. This prompted Jasmine to say she didn't think it would work because the turtles might go in different directions and that the solution would be to create a special place for them that would be long enough but that the turtles couldn't climb out of.

The teacher told the children that she would be happy to bring the turtles into the class if they could figure out a way to accurately race them. Students excitedly began yelling out ideas. One student suggested using construction paper to make a road on the floor for the turtles to crawl on. Another student suggested that they cut up cardboard boxes and tape them together to create a "turtle raceway." Still another thought the whole class might want to be involved and they could treat the turtles like mice and make an actual maze for them to go through.

The next day the turtles arrived. Adam suggested that they build multiple mazes for the turtles and make a contest out of it. He thought it would be fun if each group was given the same exact materials and allowed to build whatever kind of maze they wanted, as long as the turtles could fit through it. The children formed their own groups and began to make sketches of what they wanted their mazes to look like. For the next several weeks recess time was spent constructing turtle mazes.

This "conviction" that math is everywhere helps to empower students by enabling them to experience mathematical agency and instinctively helps them to value mathematics. As students solve problems they take on habits of mathematicians (Rowan & Bourne, 1994) and become more confident in their ability to find solutions to their own questions. These third graders used linear and time measurement, reasoning, and problem-solving skills to come up with suitable solutions to their own turtle maze constructions. Mathematicians solve problems in much the same way. They wonder, reflect, share their thinking with other interested thinkers, and test out their ideas. Providing support for young learners to engage their minds in this way helps them to believe they can solve problems.

One learning objective in my course syllabus of a graduate math methods course is that students will begin to see their world filled with mathematical wonder and problems to be solved. I ask students to put on a mathematical lens in which to view the everyday activities of their lives. A vignette from Ellen's reflective journal shows how students begin to discover mathematics in their lives in new ways.

I want to talk about my marathon training and the daily struggle of trying to convert time, distance, and speed (without a pedometer) while keeping track of my total mileage and time exercising each week. I find myself keeping a running journal because all of the figures I need are too much to keep track of in my head. Also in my running journal I record a list of all the foods I have eaten on certain days, in an effort to make sure my body is getting 55% carb, 30% protein, and 15% other stuff. (I have to have some place to splurge!) Anyway, preparing for the run has involved much more conversion and math than I tend to recognize and that's only one project.

real life math

I now wonder what other projects in my life involve thinking and using math concepts so much? Knitting with the number of stitches? Yoga with the time/pose, shopping with discounts, bill paying, and budget keeping are much more obvious. Vacation and weekend planning. The expense of living in New York City and the decisions that come with that: to take a cab or the subway, to buy or bring lunch, to scour stores for the best prices, to calculate if that is really the best use of time, etc.

Throughout this book you will find parents, students, teachers, and administrators sharing their awareness of how mathematics is a part of the lives they all live. It is a continuous metatheme of each chapter—without a personal responsiveness to the mathematics in our lives, it will be difficult to awaken a mathematical excitement and relevance in our students.

The children's story *Math Curse*, by Jon Scieszka and Lane Smith, tells of a child who suddenly sees everything in life as a math problem. How many minutes until the bus comes, which size pizza is largest, and how to divide classroom cupcakes evenly are all conundrums for the storyteller. The children's tale is a humorous way to open young eyes for viewing surroundings and everyday events mathematically. Helping children to believe their world is filled with mathematical ideas is essential to helping them become confident problem solvers and mathematical thinkers.

A Conviction That Everyone's Voice Counts

(math talk)

This is critical for students to become successful problem solvers. Also linked to this is the belief that it is through collaboration that thinking is expanded and sculpted. At the very heart of a math-infused environment is a belief about how children learn mathematics and become mathematics thinkers, confident and competent in their mathematical abilities. One cannot develop the method of questioning that includes review and the expectation that everyone has something of value to contribute if he or she believes the knowledge and power in the classroom lies solely with the teacher. This is the teaching philosophy of this work.

I believe that power and knowledge in the classroom do not lie solely with the teacher. Authority is shared and student autonomy is critical. Inclusion and engagement are reciprocal concepts. Walking into a fifth-grade classroom, I was immediately struck by the yellow construction paper banner hanging in the front of the room with bold red balloon-like lettering that read "NONE OF US IS AS SMART AS ALL OF US." A powerful message was being delivered to the students in this classroom. The implication was that everyone had a voice here in this learning community. No one person trumps the thinking of another merely by being the "smart kid." The expectation being transmitted implies that everyone has a responsibility to contribute and construct thinking in this class. Through collaboration we can create brilliance.

I was writing a collection of case studies for teachers and elementary school children about classroom dilemmas that are part of the typical school day. I authored these cases with several friends who were also teachers. The goal was to use the brief vignettes describing real life and classroom conundrums as discussion starters for students and teachers to find solutions to troublesome episodes together through discourse and problem solving. I had asked Mary, a teaching friend from Michigan, to write one and she was eager to begin. She said, "I know what my dilemma is and I know every teacher has one—the reluctant learner who tries to dismantle and undermine many of the activities as I initiate them."

Mary decided that it might be a good idea to ask Jake to co-write the vignette because he was the main character and would be the one best able to capture the perspective of the antagonist. With trepidation, she approached Jake with the project. Surprisingly, he was excited by the idea and the two of them spent one or two recess periods a week writing the story. Mary e-mailed me through-out the process, and after a few weeks I received the following message.

> Jake is no longer a problem in my class. As we began writing the case study he has felt validated with his side of the story. He has voiced his reasons for not wanting to do most of the projects I present. He says he often thinks the projects are silly and childish. Being given the opportunity to express this to me has somehow given Jake permission to participate in class projects with less opposition. I guess that it is not the case study that is beneficial for teachers and students, but the dialogue and discussion where each participant gets to honestly voice an opinion and perspective. The process has changed my teaching.

Mary explained that she now includes communication opportunities for her students through individual "chat sessions," comment cards every Friday, and group meetings. She admits that in the past she was not intentional enough in her efforts to allow each student to have a voice in the classroom. Belonging and having one's ideas valued and listened to constitute the soul of a learn-ing community. Attempting to understand the thinking of those who put forth their ideas helps us to clarify and construct our own thinking. Understanding requires listening, but listening alone does not guarantee insight. Discernment is often derived from challenging judgment, from positing possible variations on previous thought, or by being willing to toss aside a simple solution in the search for understanding of complexity or ambiguity.

A Conviction That It Takes Persistence to Solve Mathematics Problems

As teachers we often perceive our role as keeping children from frustration. It is a fine line, however, between challenge and frustration. We need to provide time and patience for our students to persist long enough to experience the joy of finishing, overcoming, or solving a challenge on their own. This process gives them the true belief in their own abilities and is much more powerful than a pat on the back from the teacher when they know they didn't come up with the solution on their own. This is what is known as mathematical agency.

When I was a fourth-grade teacher the fifth-grade teachers in my school would jokingly comment, "We can always tell which of our students were in your class last year. They are the ones who think they solve ANY problem!" Although this created laughter for the teachers' room, it is not something to make light of. As teachers, developing mathematical agency is giving children power, a power that will enable them to take risks and live in their world with mathematical confidence and competence.

A Conviction That Inquisitiveness Is the Beginning and End of Problem Solving

It is by asking that we learn. Children should be encouraged to develop their own ideas by asking questions, observing, and reasoning in the process of negotiating meaning that makes sense to them (Bruner, 1986).

I once observed a first-grade student as she approached her teacher and asked, "Miss Ellie, where do we put our math papers when we are done?" The teacher looked the student directly in the eye and responded in a matter-of-fact tone, "Tatiana, why don't you figure out a good place for our papers and then find a way to let all of us know where we need to place them when our work is finished." What this teacher was saying to Tatiana was very important: "You can figure this out and take the responsibility of informing us as a community what you have decided." The social and cultural norm of asking questions and seeking their own solutions becomes owned by students over time. The role of the teacher is to let the students know they are trusted to compose reasonable solutions to everyday problems. If we expect students to ask questions that lead to successful resolutions they will be more inclined to find problem solving an enjoyable pursuit rather than a dreaded, anxiety-producing endeavor. One cannot reason and think mathematically until the power of solving problems is viewed as an inherent activity in which students believe in their own ability to find solutions.

A Conviction That Patterns Help Us to Solve Problems

The following classroom vignette illustrates students' excitement when they discovered the beauty and order of mathematics.

Teacher: We are going to investigate consecutive numbers. Is there a series of consecutive numbers that, when added together, represent every number from 1 to 33? For example, can we represent the number 9 with a series of consecutive numbers?

Tamara: 4 + 5.

Teacher: OK. Is there another?

Sam: 2 + 3 + 4.

Teacher: Is there another?

Dianna: No.

Teacher: Let's record that as a two series and a three series of integers. How about the number 11?

Avery: 5 + 6?

Teacher: Any others?

Moses: No.

Teacher: Now continue to work in groups to see if you can represent every number from 1 to 33 with a series of consecutive numbers. Record your information on this large class chart.

	2	3	4	5	6	7
1						
2						
3						
4						
5						
6						
7						
8						
9	4 + 5	2 + 3 + 4				
10						
11	5 + 6					
12						
13						
14						
15						
16						
17						
18						
19						
20						
21						
22						
23						
24						
25						
26						
27						
28						
29						
30						
31						
32						
33						

Students work together in small groups, adding numbers as they examine each number in search of a consecutive number representation. The large class chart gradually becomes filled with the results of their work. Once the chart is completed, the teacher called the class to come and sit in clear view of the chart.

Teacher: Let's look to see if we could find a representation for each number.

The teacher circles the numbers that are left without a solution: 1, 2, 4, 8, 16, 32.

Teacher: Hmmmm. Any thoughts on where we might encounter the next integer without a series of numbers, if we were to extend this investigation further?
William: 64.
Teacher: Why do you think 64?
William: The numbers double. One doubled is two. Two doubled is four. So 32 doubled is 64.
Teacher: Are there any other patterns you notice?

Students excitedly point out patterns they observe. As students describe their patterns, the teacher circles them on the chart. If students don't see a pattern described, the teacher asks the speaker to help others understand the pattern.

Teacher: Can you explain it another way so we can see the pattern too?

This activity is a perfect example of the pattern and order of mathematics. Once students begin to realize the chart is overflowing with mathematical patterns, they start to extend the chart both vertically and horizontally, using pattern to fill it in. Then, in the same way mathematicians engage in using pattern to reach a solution, students test out their solutions to validate whether the pattern holds true for the extension. The chart remains hanging in the classroom for several weeks to allow for continuation of thinking. It is not unusual to find a student standing in front of the chart, pondering additional patterns not yet identified. In the process of constructing the large chart, students were doing addition review in a much more engaging way than being given a worksheet with problem after problem for them to solve. The consecutive number problem is not new. It is part of the *Math, A Way of Thinking* workshop and other professional development offerings. However, recognizing its value in helping students to view mathematics as a science of pattern and order (NRC, 1989) is often overlooked.

I recently had a conversation with Ilana, a graduate student, about why she had not yet had an opportunity to teach a math lesson on consecutive numbers in her student teaching placement. During her own recent participation in the consecutive number lesson, Ilana's excitement over the vast number of mathematical patterns discovered had been barely containable. She had been eager to share the lesson with her cooperating teacher and the students and was shocked to find that her cooperating teacher was less than eager about her suggestion. Ilana's discouragement was obvious as she reported the teacher's response: "I have no time for any 'extra' lessons because I am preparing students for the test."

A Conviction That Learning Is Bigger Than a Test

Ilana may have been disappointed and shocked at the teacher's response to her request, but I was outraged. The one-hour "test" referred to takes place in April and this exchange occurred in September! Are lessons and learning so scripted and scheduled that teachers become unwilling to include math experiences that fall outside of the testing preparation agenda? Clearly, this teacher was at a loss to find opportunities in the third-grade curriculum for problem solving and problem generating that go beyond the mandated assignments and topics covered on the third-grade test. Our responsibility as educators of children is to instill a love of learning that will nurture the desire to be lifelong learners, far beyond any performance on any test they may take in school.

Remember the fifth-grade classroom with the "None of Us is as Smart as All of Us" banner? The same classroom had another compelling message stapled onto the cork bulletin board on the side of the room by the class library: "Ever learning, Ever growing." Focused messages such as these can set a tone for the behavior of the classroom, but only if the messages are consistent with what goes on in the classroom. Imagine believing that learning is an endless loop of growth and discovery. I stooped next to a boy sitting in a group of students close to the message on the wall and asked what he thought the sign meant. He replied, "We're never finished with our work here. There is always something else to learn." This student recognizes the intrinsic joy in engaging in learning and solving problems. The classroom is framed around a conviction that learning has a greater value for the learners than the reward of being assessed or told they did a good job.

It is a well-documented fact that many teachers leave the profession before their third year of classroom practice. Children do not have the same option. Yet many exit their school journey feeling the effects of intrusive pressures, and this may alter their learning for a lifetime. The higher the value placed on test scores, the greater the need becomes to focus instruction on skill acquisition alone in order to pass the test. Individuality, student interest, and community relevance do not fit neatly into a test prep curriculum.

　　Preparing students to take a test at the end of the school year need not be the focus of learning all day, every day in the classroom. There are strategies for test preparation that will be discussed in chapter 9 of this book. What we need to think about is the difference between test prep learning and the deeper meaning making that results from questioning, investigating, collaborating, making connections, and being persistent. A mandated curriculum and test preparation are going to drive mathematics instruction for the foreseeable future. Scripted mathematics learning has become an insurmountable reality in most public school classrooms. This book helps teachers create a mathematics learning environment in the peripheral spaces of the classroom that values what children know and want to find out, that honors questions as evidence of learning, and that embraces the power of socially situated cognition. Teachers and pre-service teachers can work in creative ways toward meeting standards, accountability, and mathematics understanding. If the goal is to help children become concerned and informed citizens in today's world, posing questions for reflection and facilitating discussions about the thinking are critical components of the work of school.

HOW TO READ THIS BOOK

This book does not assume that realizing the conceptual convictions is easy. It does not offer a 10-step recipe for teaching and learning success. In fact, what has prompted the writing of this text is an understanding of the realities of teaching in today's schools and a desire to bring about an awareness of alternative possibilities that can foster mathematics learning "in spite of" the day-to-day pressures placed on teachers. To accomplish this is much like the task of examining one's personal financial budget. Before you can work out a spending allowance you need to determine what expenditures already exist that will influence how much is available for additional disbursement. Teachers' classrooms are not islands of autonomy. It is true one can close the classroom door and be apportioned some teaching freedom. However, increasing the episodes of teaching liberties lies in the peripheral spaces in the school day.

　　There are questions that, when investigated, may help you find those spaces beyond the influences of tight control where there is leeway to support mathematics learning that stems from concern about one's self, school, family, and community. In such a classroom community, mathematics reasoning is the expectation for all. These questions come from my own teaching experiences as well as from the professional work I participate in with parents and teachers. Each question resides in one of the obvious yet often overlooked classroom teaching places where a few small alterations can offer peripheral spaces for significant mathematics reasoning. These questions make up the chapter headings in this book. Each chapter will contain strategies for teaching to a broad range of student interests, abilities, and experiences. Activities and teaching vignettes are presented to help the reader imagine what it means to teach children mathematics that is both rigorous and engaging. In addition to the activities, research in child development and learning theory that is central to that question will be interwoven throughout each chapter.

Several of the chapters include an "authentic voice" from the field that highlights the ideas presented such as the one shared below. These letters support the convictions presented throughout the chapters and provide additional perspectives on the importance of helping young learners to become confident and competent mathematical problem solvers. Throughout the book all names are pseudonyms with the exception of the "authentic voices" whose names are as authentic as their voices.

This first "authentic voice" is particularly poignant for me as it is a keynote address given by my son to a group of college students aspiring to be successful businessmen. Nathan's honest accounting of his educational history gives new meaning to the convictions outlined in chapter 1, and draws our attention to the underlying purpose of this book: the need to emphasize critical thinking in school. Especially heartening is his accounting of the role of persistence in the journey to getting his business started. Nate wholeheartedly endorses the notion that challenging one's thinking is a lifelong endeavor and not merely a test-taking skill. His words bring to the fore our responsibility to lay the groundwork for this at an early age.

The question Nathan posed in his speech regarding how to build his business—"Where does an entrepreneur start?"—is the same as questions we ask about teaching and learning: "Where does a learner start?" or "Where does a teacher start?" The answer is the same for all three of the questions—where he is, where the learner is, where the teacher is.

"Taking Risks"
Address by Nathan McKelvey, USC Marshall
International Case Competition, February 17, 2006

Hello everyone and good evening. My name is Nate McKelvey. I'm the CEO, president, and founder of Jets International. It's an honor and a thrill to be here tonight. I also feel honored that our company is the focus of your business challenge today. Participation in the Marshall International Case Competition is a great distinction and a supreme challenge.

I think that the most exciting aspect of the competition—beyond gathering talented young people together from around the world—is that it gives the participants an opportunity to challenge existing business models. There's no right or wrong answer—just creative thinking to tackle problems—and that's what's wonderful about it. Shaking up the status quo and taking risks is the lifeblood of entrepreneurship.

It's rare to find an opportunity of this kind in an educational setting. In fact, I wish that I had been given more opportunities in school that encouraged taking risks and thinking creatively. I truly believe that it might have changed the course of my educational experience, and made the road that I traveled much more positive and rewarding.

I graduated in the bottom 30% of my class. It became apparent that if I did not attend prep school I would not be accepted to a four-year college. I attended a one-year prep school and then attended the University of Massachusetts at Amherst. You are probably thinking it was smooth sailing from this point forward. Not even close. I rarely attended classes and partied way too much. I flunked out at the end of my sophomore year. As you can imagine, my parents had had it with me by then. They were finished paying for my education, and I knew that it was now or never. I knew this was a turning point. What I didn't know at the time was this experience would turn out to be the best thing that ever happened to me.

Are you familiar with the expression, "the point of no return"? It originated as a technical term in air navigation. It refers to the point on a flight at which a plane has just enough fuel to return to the airfield it departed from. Beyond this point, you can't turn back. You have no other choice but to proceed to another destination. It's an irrevocable commitment.

During a year-long hiatus from university study, I worked two full-time jobs—at a grocery store during the day and managing a gas station at night. I saved everything I could in the hope of returning to school the following fall. After returning, a year later, to UMass, I made the Dean's list twice, and graduated two years later with a degree in economics.

So, why the big change? It wasn't just returning to college with a new attitude that altered the course of my life for the next 15 years. It was the experience I gained during the year I spent away from school. Never had I excelled as well or as consistently as I had while working. I loved the challenges of work, of finding creative ways to be more productive, efficient, and profitable. Little did I know that it would be those interests and motivations that would largely drive me to the place where I now am.

After graduation I worked for a local aircraft management company and obtained my private pilot's license. I also took evening classes at a local university in computer programming. Like many other people during this time, I had aspirations of building a dotcom business and was naïve enough to believe that one great idea would be enough to make me very successful.

My original idea was to consolidate aircraft availability information by hooking into many aircraft management companies' aircraft schedule boards across the country and organize the information to make it easily searchable—primarily for empty leg flight segments where an aircraft is traveling empty to pick up or drop off passengers. I would then resell this information to retail charter brokers. I took my business plan to a series of venture capital firms who all said basically the same thing: "You have a great idea, but you have nothing but this piece of paper."

Where does an entrepreneur start? *You start exactly where you are.* So, I built a very simple Microsoft Access program myself and I approached the venture capital firms again. This time, I received a different response: "You have a great idea, but you have no customers."

I persevered over the years, continually changing my business model to stay ahead of the competition and to meet customer needs. My company began with no revenues and was supported almost completely by my wife's modest salary. I had one programmer—me; one sales person—also me; and one employee—my sister in-law.

In 2001, the company produced $1.2 million in sales. I hired my first two salespeople and stepped up my online marketing. In 2002, sales jumped to $6.7 million. By 2005, the company generated over $17 million in sales and won the no. 66 spot in the *Inc 500* for the fastest growing companies in the United States, and was no. 1 in the transportation category.

By the way I've discovered that my story is common among entrepreneurs. A couple of years ago, I joined an EO (Entrepreneurs' Organization) group. I thought I was a wise, one-of-a-kind, out-of-the-box thinker. When I joined EO, I heard many, very similar stories. Most of the entrepreneurs I know did not do well with written tests, which often just measure how well one can regurgitate the teacher's "right" answer. It's dull, boring, and does not encourage the students to think on their own or take risks. To challenge a teacher's knowledge or authority risks being labeled as stubborn, difficult, or having a diagnosis of attention deficit disorder. I am constantly challenging my answers, digging deeper, and learning all I can as I continue to grow our company. In short, if you don't allow your ideas to be challenged, you will never learn. I know I don't have all the answers. There are always new ways to look at problems—which is why I am thrilled to hear your ideas.

As we continue to learn and refine our process, our business continues to accelerate. Our first quarter 2006 numbers have us on track to grow 80% this year. In the future, Jets International will hire and train only the best and brightest in the industry. And we will continue to educate our clients to the importance of safety and quality when selecting a private jet provider.

My thirst for learning has never been greater, which is why I am here today. I am not here to give you a recipe for being successful in the business world. I am here to listen and learn from *you*. Your talent and perseverance brought you here. Whoever wins or loses tonight, remember—it's inconsequential. What matters is that you are taking risks and applying your creativity. I was told many times that my ideas had no merit. If you truly believe in your ideas and have the will and motivation to succeed, no one can stand in your way.

Thank you again for inviting me to be here with you tonight.

At the conclusion of each chapter will be a Teacher as Researcher Thoughts section. Here, additional questions are posed for the reader to ponder. These "action research" suggestions are meant to support a move in the teaching and learning experience from a series of conundrums to new heights of possibilities for teacher as researcher and child as learner. Remaining curious and modeling what it looks like to be a lifelong learner help to promote the notion of teaching and learning that underlies this book. It is hypocritical of us to expect our students to be curious and ask questions about their learning but to remain content with what we know. This section is the chance for teachers to reflect on their own practice and raise their own questions to think about in more depth. A teacher's questions of practice might stem from a range of classroom experiences and events—a student who doesn't seem to understand, a lesson that goes badly, unsatisfactory interactions with parents, poor communications with colleagues, a student's wonderment, the need to better understand your own teaching behavior, or the desire to motivate student learning are but a few instances that might provoke further investigation.

CHAPTER QUESTIONS

Chapter 2, "What Does the Room Teach?" examines physical space and the ways in which the room design may increase or detract from mathematics learning. The chapter includes ideas for how to turn room arrangement, wall space, and organization of materials into learning opportunities and community-building experiences. The teacher isn't the only learning specialist in the room—the room itself is a teacher of students as well. Its style can be subtle, as in where and how materials are stored, or more blatantly instructive, as in the arrangement of desks. Examples from teachers who have worked with students to provide alternative learning spaces will provide for discussion and reflection. Also included will be a case study of one teacher who taught both a regular classroom of students and an after-school class with some of the same students. The differences in student engagement and motivation, as well as distinct variations in the teacher's pedagogy will be discussed. A physical space inventory will be presented to assist teachers in taking stock of their classrooms and finding their own ways to use space in more creative, collaborative, instructive ways for mathematics learning.

Chapter 3, "Who Asks the Questions? Who Answers Them?" includes a student vignette of a project on "why kids fight." A discussion follows this vignette regarding the importance of listening to student questions and strategies that help students shape their questions into problems to be solved. As teachers, if we ask less and listen more a whole new classroom energy emerges. Underlying this reality is a belief and trust that students can ask questions that will lead to new understandings and promote increased interest in learning.

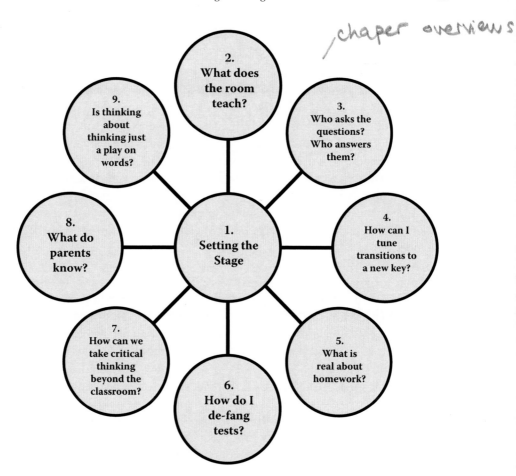

chaper overviews

Figure 1.1 Chapter questions.

Included in this chapter is a study by a graduate student on how to increase student-to-student dialogue during problem-solving discussions. Problem solving and problem posing, reasoning and analysis, and application to real-world situations are the heart of mathematics learning. This chapter examines ways to make these skills organic rather than confining them to a list that hangs on the classroom wall.

Chapter 4, "How Can I Tune Transitions to a New Key?" considers ways in which transitions can be transformed into enjoyable, learning-rich intervals that are also mathematical in nature. Ending one lesson and segueing into another is often a disruptive experience that takes up too much classroom time and causes frustration for many teachers and students. Facilitating the transition in the morning from home to the classroom, switching between subject lessons, moving from the classroom into other school spaces, and end-of-the-day fidget time all are explored to find learning opportunities grounded in mathematics that are more than crowd-control events. Examples are provided that highlight how a daily attendance graph can create lively discussions and how math games can fill the lost moments between subjects in ways that will capture student attention in nondirective, supportive ways.

Chapter 5, "What Is Real about Homework?" examines what math homework might look like if we abandon the usual repetitious, meaningless problems and look for new ideas to make the homework experience meaningful and more engaging, relative, and interactive for students. Suggestions and examples are offered that will have students wanting to do homework and begging for more. This chapter looks at the reasons why homework is assigned, what research and theory tell us about what makes homework an effective instructional tool, and when it is detrimental to children's learning. Also discussed will be alternate ways to conceptualize the ritual of homework and parents' perspectives on homework.

Chapter 6, "How Do I De-Fang the Test?" considers test preparation strategies to incorporate on a daily basis that are not intrusive and still provide math skill review. These examples are from teachers who created classrooms filled with project learning that sometimes deviates from, yet still maintains, the integrity of the mandated curriculum schedule. The chapter accentuates the importance of making parents partners in helping to ready the children for tests, as well as looking at what can be done in the weeks prior to taking a test that will make the test-taking day a more relaxed experience for all involved.

Chapter 7, "How Can We Take Critical Thinking Beyond the Classroom?" explores projects for use with the entire school community. When the whole school works together to focus on critical thinking the culture of learning shifts from a pressure-filled test preparation ethos to one of collaboration. Taking math fusion beyond the individual classroom into the hall, outside on the playground, and creating whole-school learning events sends the message to students that problem solving and critical thinking are important skills. Classrooms where students play together with the same sense of purpose as they work together are shared. This chapter explores ways for teachers and students to explore mathematics in spaces outside of school walls and looks at the learning value in a kickball game, a schoolwide graphing or measurement project, or a jump rope competition. Strategies will also be shared for bringing mathematics reasoning into interdisciplinary settings, as well as suggestions for community outreach possibilities.

Chapter 8, "What Do Parents Know?" accentuates how parents can help us to understand children and how to build a parent–teacher connection that is positive and supporting. The learning and assessment puzzle is not complete without the parent perspective piece. Examples from documented parent interviews uncover the value of parents as an untapped resource. This chapter illuminates parent desires, anxieties, and strategies that work in the home, as well as what parents need from teachers and schools to help them help their children. Suggestions are provided for interacting with parents to make math learning in the home and classroom more than "practice the times tables with flashcards." Some examples of questions to ponder and ideas for action research are:

What are parents really asking me?

What are the ways I reach out to parents?

What is the nature of the talk about parents in the teachers' room?

How can I use what parents provide?

Chapter 9, "Is Thinking about Thinking Just a Play on Words?" looks at the research that supports reflection as an integral learning component and provides a guide to help students learn how to write reflectively about their mathematics thinking. Research on how reflection increases learning is presented. Student math journal entries will be shared that demonstrate the learning possibilities of student reflections. These journal entries draw attention to the role that teacher guidance, reflection, and response plays in this process. One classroom set of student math journal reflections, written over several months, will provide insight into the process of developing student reflective thinking.

These chapters, taken together, demonstrate how learning mathematics that stems from wonderment and intellectual curiosity can occur within the teaching and learning spaces of an elementary school classroom. Such math infusion may capture and transform mechanically compliant students into learners instilled with a need to know and find out, to make sense of that which intrigues, and to be more intelligent risk takers. Mathematics reasoning serves as the fulcrum point for learning in an abundance of peripheral spaces while still meeting the demands of curriculum, accountability, and the expectations of parents and administrators.

Chapter 2

What Does the Room Teach?

Welcome to Room 305

On the opening day of school, children were greeted with blank walls as they walked into Room 305 for the first time. Ms. Thibideau smiled as students glanced about the room with curiosity and amazement. Every conceivable wall space in Ms.Thibideau's third-grade classroom was sectioned off into 28 different polygon shapes— rectangles, squares, triangles, even a trapezoid or two. Below are examples of the divided bulletin boards.

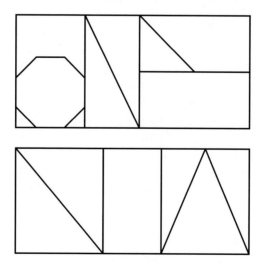

Once students were situated in their seats Ms. Thibideau carried out the routines of attendance and lunch count. She then introduced a lesson planned to build a sense of community and collaboration with the students.

management

She asked them to form in groups of three. In their groups, students were to comment about the wall spaces.

"Talk together about the following question: What do you think of the spaces?"

As she walked among the groups Ms. Thibideau heard a variety of student commentary on the subject of the bulletin board displays or lack thereof.

"Why aren't there any bulletin boards up?"

"The spaces are all shapes."

"Yeah, some of them are funny shapes."

"Which ones are funny?"

"The room looks empty."

"The ones on that wall all fit together with no spaces left on the outside or between."

Ms. Thibideau interjected as she listened in: "Do you mean the octagons and trapezoids?"

"Yeah, I forgot what you called them."

After asking for their attention, Ms. Thibideau poses a new question. "Are the shapes all the same size?"

Students laugh and say in unison, "NO. There are squares and rectangles and different shapes."

"I mean, are some shapes bigger than others? Do they take up more space than others, do they have the same area or are their areas different? Do some of the shapes have more room inside them than others? If they were all fenced-in yards for your pet dog, would some of the fenced-in spaces have more room for your dog to run around in than others?"

The chatter in the room began to increase as students huddled together in their small groups to discuss the question posed. Ms. Thibideau directed the groups to take some time to investigate the question of whether or not any shapes were bigger than others. The students were to use any strategy they wanted to but they must work in a group of three to solve the problem.

Students spent the next 30 minutes actively involved in solving this problem. One group of students decides to cut out paper squares the same size as the square and begin by checking if all the squares are equal in size. Once they conclude the squares are the same they cut up the paper squares and proceed to cover the rectangles with the pieces. They decide the rectangles are also the same size. This causes a discussion between two students. "I think we did it wrong. The rectangles look bigger than the squares." "No, they are longer, but skinnier. See." The student goes up to the board with the rectangle and shows that the shorter side is smaller than any side on the square. "Ohhhhh, the longer side makes up for the shorter side, so they equal out." "Yeah."

The group proceeds to the trapezoid and uses the same method of cutting up their original square shape into smaller pieces that fit inside the

hard when not understand math... colaboration

trapezoid perfectly. Now they begin to speculate that all shapes are going to be the same size and hurry over to the triangles.

Another group of three students uses a completely different approach. These students make paper copies of the shapes and divide each shape into small squares by drawing grids on the shapes. They proceed to count the small squares inside each shape. The group is about to declare that all shapes are the same size when they realize the octagon does not fit their conjecture. After more discussion the students determine the octagon has 10 more squares. Members of the group are excited that they have found the exception and begin to whisper so other groups will not overhear what they have discovered.

A third group argued that a dog didn't have as much space to run in the triangular shapes because of the corners. "But there are four corners in the square and rectangle, and only three in the triangle." "I know but the triangle corners are pointier and don't have as much room." "I think they are the same. Same space. A small dog could have as much running space in both."

Ms. Thibideau calls the groups to the rug area and asks for a group to share their thinking. The first group who used the paper cutouts declares, "All the shapes are equal in space." Ms. Thibideau asks them to explain to the rest of the class why they think so and they show the class their reasoning by taking the cut-up squares around to each of the other shapes, showing how the pieces fit.

The grid group can hardly contain themselves with their discovery. They exclaim, "The octagon shape is biggest. It has 10 more small squares."

This vignette illustrates a way to use the classroom as a means to invite discussion, encourage questions, and infuse mathematics learning on the very first day of school. Many students enter on the first day of school into classrooms adorned with colorful bulletin boards constructed over the summer by eager and dedicated teachers. After the first day, however, these painstakingly decorated spaces attract very little, if any, attention from students. Even those bulletin boards designed to teach, such as "6 Steps to Solving Problems," or boards that send "I'm glad you're here" messages such as "Welcome to Room 207" with apple cutouts scattered under and on a tree, each with a name or photo of the newly arriving students, have a brief attention-getting life span. Students in Ms. Thibideau's classroom learn from the first day of school that this classroom will be a place for their questions and group dialogue. They ascertain that the room itself will hold opportunities for learning. They realize their teacher listens and asks questions more than she talks or tells. They learn that this classroom expects engagement.

how?

Ms. Thibideau followed this lesson with a homework assignment. Students were told to choose one of the wall spaces as their own and to find a way to

try! listen & question

designate their shape space with their name. By the end of the week each student was to decorate his or her shape with a collage of artifacts from home. They could attach anything to the space that represented something about themselves as long as the item could fit into the space without crossing onto another student's space. Ms. Thibideau participated in this activity and created a trapezoid space for herself. She decorated her trapezoid with pictures of her four children and two grandchildren. She cut out a picture from a magazine of a sailboat and a map of Block Island, Rhode Island. A list of show tunes and a menu from Alfonso's Restaurant also filled her space. An Almond Joy wrapper was attached.

On Friday, students were asked to find three people who have something in common with them. "The ways we are similar" was the topic for discussion at morning meeting. The bulletin boards took on new life each day because Ms Thibideau utilized them with new questions or tasks for the students:

- Students pick a name out of a hat and interview that person about his or her space and then introduce that person to the class.
- Artifact treasure hunt: Who likes soccer? Find the teddy bear. Who has been to San Francisco?
- Write three questions you want to ask three different people about their board space.
- In small groups, collect information from the boards and find a way to represent the data for the rest of the class.

In the process, the class in Room 305 developed into a community of learners who discovered ways they are alike as well as ways they are unique. Their teacher is a participator in the community who shares her interests and curiosities with the students in the same manner she expects of her students. Ms. Thibideau does not set herself aside as the authority figure in the classroom but sets up the learning for the students to participate in. She does establish herself as the person who provides opportunity, motivation, space, and boundaries for learning and the building of relationships that includes everyone, even herself.

ROOM ARRANGEMENT

You walk into a room and see row after row of desks, all facing straight ahead at the teacher and whiteboard. Several people are already sitting silently in scattered seats throughout the room. Contrast this with the experience of entering a second room where the desks are positioned in groups of four with baskets filled with crayons, pencils, markers, and tape in the center of each grouping. The teacher's desk is inconspicuously placed against the wall, off to the side of the room. A few children are already seated and talking with one another. The

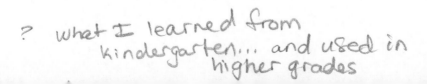

first classroom says: We are serious and will do our work individually and look to the teacher for guidance. The second classroom says: We are ready for work and will be expected to talk with one another and collaborate.

There is nothing wrong with being serious about one's work or about working independently. Yet if the first message you send to children is one of individualism and separateness, it becomes the classroom culture to work alone to get your work done. We know from research that creativity and thinking are enhanced when ideas are shared and discourse around divergent understandings occurs. Sharing one's thinking and asking others about their ideas are life skills that help our students learn to be critical thinkers. What does this mean? Is there another way to think about this? If this is true, then maybe _____ is also true. "What if" and "I wonder" become part of the conversational lexicon in the classroom. Asking others to clarify their thinking or to help you understand something that is unclear is the way we, as adults, develop and grow our own thinking. Biases often stem from the recycling of old thinking without other points of view or ideas surfacing and being pondered and explored.

My goal as a teacher has been and continues to be to create a classroom where children are working to "get smart" rather than to "look smart." Carol Dweck eloquently explains the difference in her book *Self-Theories: Their Role in Motivation, Personality, and Development* (2000). According to Dweck, looking smart is when students want to get the "A" because an A tells the world you are brilliant. "Getting smart" is when you learn because you want to know. Schools are structured to have students "look smart." You have achieved the highest level of knowing and are smarter than anyone who received less than an A. Teachers routinely ask questions that require one right answer, and they question children until a student comes forth with that "correct" answer. The motivation for learners is not to learn but to "get it right" or make the teacher, the other students, and parents think they "get it." Listen to any group of teachers conversing about students for more than five minutes and the phrase "He or she 'gets it' or 'doesn't get it'" will come up in the exchange. It is our national teaching culture to lead students to the "right answer" (Stigler & Hiebert, 1999). Our national image of teaching is that the teacher's job is to make it as easy as possible for students to "get it."

In the process of making learning easy and painless we deny students the learning revenue gained from struggling with an idea or a problem. Discovering a solution or creating understanding as a result of personal intellectual thrashing about is the stuff that builds confidence and competence. It is how children engage in learning to get smart instead of learning merely to look smart. As teachers, our role is to provide opportunities for children to wonder and be curious. Such intrinsic motivation stems from that which interests them, motivation that originates from their everyday lives and things that have a direct influence on their lives. Learning because you are genuinely interested in finding out is very different from learning to please a teacher or to get a good grade. One has the long-term effect of creating boredom with the process of learning and the other has the potential to produce lifelong learners who find pleasure and satisfaction in seeking out answers to that which makes them wonder.

WHAT DOES LEARNING TO GET SMART LOOK LIKE?

A final project assignment I give to graduate students who are learning to become teachers is to find an area of mathematics teaching or learning that holds some degree of fascination for them. It might be something in mathematics they have feared or struggled with; it may be a question that has arisen for them since they have started to visualize themselves as teachers of mathematics; or it may be something they find intriguing and would like to explore. The assignment is initially met with confusion and skepticism and I am confronted with a million questions: What do we need to hand in to you? Do we have to write a paper and how long should it be? What must our "presentation" to the class look like? It takes a great deal of explanation and reassurance to convince the students that this is about what they want and need to know and find out and not what they need to do to please me or complete my list of requirements. The assignment is about their learning journey rather than about the final product. I want students to encounter learning and be infected by the pure joy of the experience. My aspiration is for them to be inquisitive and to let their curiosity drive them to new and previously unknown places. The "presentations" take the form of sharing their excitement or newfound knowledge with the rest of the class in much the same way they might communicate an experience of learning how to ski with friends or other interested people. We learn new things every day and it is not common for any of us to share this learning by writing a 10-page paper with references and footnotes. I do ask that if students come across something they deem might be useful for the rest of us that they please make copies to share.

Amy's Final Learning Journey Project

Amy is one graduate student and the following story is her description of the learning journey she undertook as she grappled with this final project assignment. Though the topic of the learning is well beyond what an elementary school student might research, the story is being shared as an example of what learning for learning's sake might look like in any classroom. The resulting learning benefits would be similar for younger students or adults. Here is Amy's journey in her words.

I started my research by looking up topics on the Web that I had previously studied regarding math in nature. I remember having learned about the Fibonacci Series and its relationship to the arrangement of leaves on a plant in high school, but I did not remember the particulars involved. I started my journey looking for any and all articles on the Fibonacci Series, glancing at some, attempting to read others. While I found some of the information interesting, nothing really jumped out to me enough to look into more deeply. I moved on to looking for articles on angles in nature, including the angles of tree branches and of birds in flight. Again, I found a few articles, some of which were worth a glance, but none that truly piqued my interests. I decided to try one more time to find a more interesting subject concerning math in nature and searched for "animal spot patterns." I had expected to find some information on whether or not animals' spots or stripe patterns are at all consistent, or if there is some sort of mathematical concept behind what patterns animal spots or stripes create. What I found instead was the mathematical formula that describes the biological process by which an animal embryo gets its spot or stripe pigments in the womb. This discovery would direct me down one of the most purely self-motivated paths to learning I have ever experienced.

I uncovered an article, "How the Leopard Got its Spots," by Lewis Dartnell that presents two differential equations originally developed by mathematician Alan Turing that may describe how animal embryos develop the elaborate fur patterns exhibited in nature. Though Dartnell presents this complicated mathematical theory rather clearly, I found myself reading the article over and over, stopping after each paragraph to try to wrap my head around all of the information I had just read. Even after reading the article several times, drawing diagrams and notes for myself to help me conceptualize these concepts, and staring at photographs of patterned animals for some form of intellectual inspiration, I still do not completely understand Turing and Dartnell's theory and have many questions about the information that I want to have answered. However, the parts of the theory that I was able to interpret truly fascinated me.

Inside animal embryos, there are two chemicals: one is called the activator (A) and one is called the inhibitor (I). The activator stimulates the production both of itself and of the inhibitor. The inhibitor suppresses the production both of itself and of the activator.

There is a mathematical formula that represents the increases and decreases in the embryo's activator and inhibitor chemicals and it can be written as follows:

$$\frac{dA}{dt} = f(A, I) + \frac{d^2 A}{dx^2}$$

$$\frac{dI}{dt} = g(A, I) + d\frac{d^2 I}{dx^2}$$

Amy went on to explain how the formula applies to color pigmentation on different animals, as well as differences in coloring on individual animals. She explained to the class how she now understood why her cat had orange stripes on the tail and orange spots on the rest of the body. Amy was clearly excited by her learning and shared some of her new questions with us:

> Why do some big animals, like zebras and tigers have stripes while some smaller animals, like house cats, have spots? In the same way, why do giraffes have blocks of color instead of tiny spots? I also wonder how animals of the same species get different patterns of stripes and spots, such as zebras whose stripes are as unique as our fingerprints. In the future, I would love to learn more about how this theory would answer my questions.

Amy wrote the following in her final self-assessment for the course:

> While the information I learned about how the patterning of embryos can possibly be explained by a mathematical formula was truly mind-boggling, I feel that the bigger lesson I learned in doing this research project involves what I believe to be learning in its purest form. The guidelines and instructions for this project were left wide open, almost too much so, I felt at first, for my borderline control freak personality. I usually like to be told exactly what my teacher expects of me before starting a project, and I believe this would have translated into my own future teaching. However, it was truly the freedom allowed in this assignment that encouraged me to struggle through the initial aimless wandering phase into investigating, discovering, and intellectualizing simply for the true interest and curiosity I had about the subject matter. I learned more about the topic at hand and myself as a learner and future teacher in this one, entirely open-ended research project than I ever learned in any of the countless research-based projects I've done in my long educational career. What is truly amazing to me is that our professor had little to no control over what we were investigating, how we were conducting our research, or what form our final presentations would take. Whereas I always felt that teaching would mean me having to guide my students step by step into new understandings, I learned that some of the deepest and most substantial learning of all can, and should, take place by the learner, for the learner's sake. While I now feel privileged in knowing that one of nature's most alluring spectacles, the patterns of animal spots and stripes, may be a very mathematical phenomenon, I believe that my newfound perspective on

motivating students to learn for learning's sake will have a profound effect on my future teaching practices.

Amy's learning experience exemplifies learning to "get smart." She let her own curiosity drive the pathway of her discoveries and she did not merely look up information to meet a teacher's requirement for research. Though it is almost impossible to allow an "Amy experience" for every classroom assignment, I believe there needs to be more of a balance between having students comply and follow teacher and textbook instructions to the letter and providing spaces for students to truly research that which interests or intrigues them. This is when students can begin to differentiate for themselves what constitutes learning and what it feels like to discover and learn because you want to know. It is only then that we are modeling for children the joys and euphoria of life-long learning. Without such experiences, many children leave school with an attitude that learning is over and now I can get on with "real life."

Meg's Story

I want you to meet Meg. She was a graduate student who did her student teaching in a fourth-grade classroom. Her cooperating teacher's name was Eileen, and Eileen also used her classroom to teach the *In Addition* math program.

The *In Addition* After School Mathematics Initiative is an inquiry-based approach to learning mathematics beyond the classroom. The design of *In Addition* and the components of the program are intended to work in unique and innovative ways for children to learn mathematics in an afterschool setting.

Traditionally, afterschool programs are designed for students to get help with their homework, be tutored in a particular subject, or participate in recreational activities. *In Addition* is built to encourage an excitement for learning by providing students with stimulating experiences that draw on their interests and ideas. Students use these experiences as a springboard to ask questions and conduct mathematics investigations that connect to their family, school, and the urban environment in which they live.

The *In Addition* program has serviced children and their families for 4 years and has been situated in three public urban elementary schools. Children are randomly selected from a pool of interested students in grades 3, 4, and 5 at each school. The program takes place three days a week, Tuesday through Thursday from 3:00 to 5:00. The program is taught either by a graduate student or by a classroom teacher from one of the participating schools. The primary focus of the *In Addition* program is to foster critical thinking and to work at building relationships among students and their parents and the *In Addition* staff. The goal of the program is to help students and parents become mathematically competent and confident as they explore the relevance of mathematics to their lives.

Two of the girls in Eileen's regular fifth-grade classroom, Janine and Delia, were also participants in the *In Addition* program after school. Meg became intrigued with the interactions and learning of these two girls and the differences in demeanor of the girls between the two settings. Here is the story in Meg's own words.

Throughout this semester I had been student teaching not only in a fifth-grade classroom, but also in *In Addition*: An After School Program in Mathematics. These two classes were taught by the same teacher, Eileen, but somehow managed to be two completely different environments for learning. Both the afterschool program and the fifth-grade class take place each day in the same classroom. The fifth-grade classroom consists of 24 students ranging in age from 10 to 13, because a few of the students have been retained in earlier grades. The school contains a "Talented and Gifted" class at each grade, creating a system of tracking students. Students remain with the same group of students throughout their elementary school years at this school. The afterschool program is open to students in grades 3 through 5, ranging in ages from 8 to 11. Students are chosen by a lottery system open to any child who applies. Each year the program chooses 7 students from each grade, 3, 4, and 5. Although there are only 21 boys and girls in the afterschool program the class is much more diverse, containing students from both the "Gifted and Talented" classes and regular classrooms. Therefore the students do not all know each other as well as the fifth graders.

The classroom is rather small to accommodate the 24 students in the fifth-grade class, but what it lacks in space it makes up for in light, with windows covering two sides of the classroom. There are 11 rectangular student tables formed into three groups and a 12th table that is smaller and round at the back of the room. Two students sit at each table, so with the round table there is barely enough space for our entire class. Most of the lessons taught are on the rug that is located in the far corner of the classroom. Students spend about 20 minutes at a time seated on the rug listening to lessons. The students appear to find it uncomfortable to sit on the rug, as they squirm and wiggle about. However, the principal believes it is important for students to sit on the rug for class discussions, even though some students are 13 years old.

During the school day Eileen often appeared frustrated and angry with the class. Time and again she would be frequently interrupted by students who were not paying attention, walking about the room, fighting, or talking among themselves. Eileen often raised her voice in order to get their

rug good... A. I think... when... how?

sometimes have to...

attention and would stop lessons in order to regain student attention. She habitually sent students to the office for refusing to comply with her requests to quiet down or to stop distracting other students. In the beginning of the day she always started out ready to teach the planned lessons, but by lunch time her frustrations bubbled over. The class would come crashing up the stairs, excited after spending time in the yard during recess. Students were still discussing who won dodgeball and who was gossiping about whom. Eileen's many attempts to calm them down seemed fruitless. On the toughest days the read-aloud that followed lunch was cut short and little was accomplished during the lesson that would follow. The class just seemed incapable of getting it together. Eileen and I often shared looks of sheer frustration. At these times, Janine participated in the rowdiness of the class, yet Delia would sit with a look similar to the one Eileen and I sported.

Eileen and I often commented on our desire for the school day to end so we could get to after school. We both agreed that teaching after school was fun and surprisingly relaxing after what was so often a frustrating day with our fifth graders. I was surprised that I actually looked forward to spending another two hours at the school following the end of the school day. I needed to understand why I felt so differently about these two classes.

I initially observed that Janine acted very differently within the two environments. During school she was often argumentative and disrespectful, but during the afterschool program she was polite and delightful in her personal conversations as well as during group discussions. I was perplexed by the fact that one teacher could be teaching two such different classes, in the same day, in the same classroom, and could create such different reactions from a student.

The classroom completely changes during afterschool time. I immediately noticed a difference in how members of this group functioned with one another. Students talked together and listened to each other. Students were still very active, but somehow they managed to have conversations where they built on the ideas of others. Not only did these students listen to each other, but Eileen was more relaxed during this part of the day, as well. She still required students to walk quietly to and from the playground, but it became more of a game. Rather than simply telling them they needed to be quiet or demanding quiet, Eileen modeled quiet. When afterschool test prep sessions were being held in the library she asked all her students to walk on tip toe through the hallway so as not to create a distraction, leading the line herself in an exaggerated tip toe. When she wanted them to talk quietly during snack time she would often say, "Oh I had such a long day, can we try to talk quietly so I can relax?" This is not to say that *In Addition* was never a rowdy place, but it was never out of control.

Eileen routinely joked with the students and took the first 15 minutes of afterschool time to sit and relax with them. I noticed that as she relaxed the tension also left Delia's face. I wondered if Janine was also sensing the change in Eileen's and my attitudes at the end of the day.

Eileen and I frequently spent time informally discussing the differences we experienced between regular class time and the afterschool program. She talked about how tired she was of raising her voice with the students in the fifth-grade class and how she wished there was a way for her to get their attention. No matter what she attempted, she felt the students just ignored her and that she had no choice but to yell at them. On really tough days she would confide in me that she wasn't sure how she was going to survive teaching this class any longer. We would flop into chairs after passing snack out to the afterschool students and watch them peacefully eating and talking to one another or playing games. A few of the students would ask if we had a hard day and express sympathy.

I decided one way to ascertain the differences in what students thought about their learning environments was to ask them. I spoke with Janine and asked her to tell me five things she was learning in school and five things she was learning after school. In school she listed, "Adding fractions, different poems, adding decimals, trying to stop gossip, and getting along with friends." The first three items show specific content she is being taught. In her classroom they were given formulas to use for adding fractions and decimals. They also learned how to write different poems using different rules for the structure of the poems. When she constructed the list for the afterschool learning it contained, "Work with a group, learn about our neighborhood, how to make graphs, and to do math." These lists are in contrast to one another. Students begin their research on the parks by working in groups learning about their neighborhood and gathering information. They represent the information with graphs. In the fifth-grade classroom the graphs would be created and completed in a single day, but Janine says in the afterschool program the graphing takes time for them to make and refix them to make sure they are accurate. Sometimes they have to collect more information and make new graphs. When I questioned her about "do math" she said that was the point of after school. She further explained, "We *do* the math and talk about it, not just using formulas to get answers."

I also asked Janine to draw me a picture of her school classroom (see Figure 2.1). In the picture she drew the teacher sitting on a stool with three students in front of her on the rug. Other students are located around the classroom at tables. It appears that everyone is doing something different. In her picture of after school, all the students are seated on the rug together (see Figure 2.2). It is actually impossible to determine who the teacher is in the space.

Figure 2.1

Figure 2.2

It became clear to me that I needed to interview Janine about her two school environments. During the interview she mentioned that the behavior problems in the fifth-grade class prevent students from getting their work done. Janine also reported that Eileen's mood was different in the two classes. I asked her what she meant.

Janine said, "She feels kind of mad when she's in school and tired and stuff, but then when she goes to after school she's calm and she sits down and relaxes and you know, she smiles." Janine also indicated that she thought after school was more interesting because of the projects that they work on.

During lunch one day, Janine, Delia, and I spent the entire period together with a tape recorder on the table. We sat in the classroom and talked about teaching and learning after school and in the regular classroom. The conversation began with a discussion of their ideal classroom. What would be the "best classroom you could imagine?" Immediately, without any hesitation, both girls responded, "We could chew gum." This is interesting because in the after school they are allowed to break the schoolwide rule of no gum chewing. The girls extended their imagining to the ideal teacher and said they wanted the "best" teachers. Before I could ask, they qualified "best" to mean teachers who are smart and fun: "You know, like when Eileen laughs and jokes with us."

Janine went on to explain that learning was fun when you are learning something and "playin' around with it." I asked when they "played around with learning" and Janine said that in the after school the projects helped them to learn stuff but they had time to play around with things for more time than in school. "Like our park graphs, we worked on them for a long time and it never got boring."

The girls talked about how in school they are learning to multiply fractions, but in after school they go outside and observe parks and do research. There is more time to figure out the answers in after school, more time for thinking. "In the school classroom, Eileen doesn't joke around with us as much because it is time to be serious."

When I asked them to describe the students in the ideal classroom Janine responded that it would be good if they listened to each other during discussions, but that there also needed to be a "talk time" for them so they wouldn't have to be talking during lessons. They thought that after lunch might be a good time for free talk so everyone could get their energy out and discuss things that happened at lunch. Delia thought that talk time might help students calm themselves.

"During after school we all play together as a group at the yard, but during school when we are at the yard they don't take time to run around and play because there are so many people around they don't get their energy out." When Delia describes how things in school get out of control following lunch she is describing the time of day when she tends to become frustrated. It is also the time of day when Eileen and I share similar frustrations. If Delia and Janine are to be taken seriously, it makes sense to give students some free "talk time" after returning from recess.

Meg has her own elementary school classroom now in another state yet calls or writes me from time to time to chat. Her experiences in the two learning environments with Eileen helped her to think about the ways she wanted to interact with students in her own classroom.

It is clear from Meg's depiction of the two learning environments that how we greet students, the pace at which we direct our instruction, and the opportunities we provide students to voice their perspectives on teaching behaviors are all factors in the classroom cultures that result. Given the demands of teaching in today's classrooms with the accountability bar raised so high, these may seem like inconsequential factors to many teachers. Meg's observations and research are a means for us to rethink how we structure the day and the value of seeking student voices about our own teaching. A simple activity such as "Describe your ideal teacher or ideal classroom" may provide an insightful glimpse of how our students perceive us as teachers.

What does this have to do with mathematics reasoning in the elementary school classroom? Without an environment that listens to student perspectives, and one that honors building relationships with students over all else, it becomes hypocritical to ask students to listen to each other and to build ideas from the collective and individual thinking of a community of learners. The vignettes describing the students in Ms. Thibideau's class, Amy's experience, and Delia and Janine are all stories that are grounded in student/teacher relationships. In the case of Ms. Thibideau, the story sets up an environment that says to the students, "I want you to investigate your own thinking and to question and build on the ideas of your classmates." Amy, by her own admission, would not have felt the freedom to go off on a learning journey that took her to unknown learning landscapes if she did not believe that her professor would value this type of learning trajectory. Delia and Janine teach us the importance of listening to children and how to make adjustments based on student needs. The following piece about Steven Levy's classroom provides another example of a teacher who sees the educational worth in letting the classroom belong to the students.

A ROOM WITHOUT FURNITURE

Steven Levy is an award-winning teacher who has taught elementary school for over 22 years and who was recognized as the 1992–93 Massachusetts Teacher of the Year. In his book, *Starting From Scratch*, he offers a vision for teaching elementary school students that is embraced by this author. The projects he details are embedded in the children's own interests and community, and skills are developed through project-based learning and an inquiry approach to teaching. Mr. Levy describes a first-day-of-school experience that highlights a unique classroom arrangement. On the first day of school, his class of 25 fourth-grade students walk into an empty classroom. There are no desks, chairs, or bookcases. The room is void of furniture and materials. He gathers the children on the floor and greets them. He explains that they will be designing and constructing all the furniture for their classroom. The students spend the next few weeks raising money and drawing classroom plans. Students studied furniture building, gained knowledge about investments and interest rates in order to draft loan contracts for the funders of their project, and interviewed carpenters and bankers. After one month, the classroom was on the way to being filled with designer-quality furniture that the students were building together. They acquired sophisticated mathematical knowledge of measurement, area, angles, fractions, decimals, percentages, and data collection in the process. The students became confident and competent in their ability to investigate, reason, problem solve, and make connections between the mathematics they needed to know and the mathematics they were learning.

Although possibly improbable for many teachers to find the acceptance, support, or energy to undertake a project on the scale of the one Steven Levy planned and orchestrated, there are underlying principles that any teacher can import into any classroom with a few alterations. One modification might be to provide students with a classroom that for all practical purposes is empty on the first day of school. The desks and chairs are lined up on the sides of the room and materials are in packages in a pile. Discuss with students what kind of learning space they would like. Think about how you want to work together, where it makes sense to place the supplies so that they are accessible when needed. Talk about the various spaces you might want to create to help students learn: a library, quiet space, listening area, large area for gathering as a group, spaces for drawing, writing, and reading. Have students work in small groups to create classroom design plans and then discuss them as a large group. This may seem like a lengthy process, but you are offering students choice and ownership of their classroom learning community, which has payoffs that can't be underestimated.

TEACHER AS RESEARCHER THOUGHTS

1. Try for a week to greet your students more informally. Smile and talk with them as you would your best friends—in a relaxed manner and with limited intensity. Have the focus be on them as people, not as students who need to cover material by the day's end. What changes do you notice in them? In yourself?

2. In what ways does offering your students choices in where they work alter the classroom climate?

3. In what ways does the classroom culture change when students have decision-making power about the room design?

4. Schedule a 10-minute "talk time" each day where students can talk freely with one another. Participate in this time with them by sitting and talking about anything but school with some students. After several weeks, describe what happened.

This chapter examined the physical and socio-cultural spaces of the classroom and the ways in which the room design may increase or detract from mathematics learning. It included ideas for how to turn room arrangement, wall space, and organization of materials into learning opportunities and community-building experiences. The teacher isn't the only learning specialist in the room—the room itself is a teacher of students as well. The style can be subtle, as in where and how materials are stored, or more blatantly instructive, as in the arrangement of desks.

CLASSROOM INVENTORY

This inventory is provided for you to take a personal accounting of your own classroom in order to reflect on the implicit messages you are sending your students about teaching and learning.

1. Where is the teacher's desk located?

2. Are classroom materials easily accessible to students to allow them to gather and return them without assistance from the teacher?

3. Is the work on the wall student-created?

4. Is there a large space for group meetings?

5. Are textbooks located in the reference section of the classroom library?

6. Is there evidence of student choice opportunities?

Chapter 3

Who Asks the Questions?
Who Answers Them?

How Many Grapefruit Will Fit in This Room?

Ms. Thompson posed this question to her class of fourth graders. They sat in silence for a minute as they stared at her. The questions then began to flow—"How are we suppose to figure that out?" "Can we use yardsticks?" "What size are the grapefruit?"

Ms. Thompson put the class into six groups of four or five students each and told them to work at solving this problem. Initially, the student talk was about the impossible problem. Then came the inevitable: "Do you know the answer?" Ms. Thompson jokingly replied, "Of course, I brought in a truckload of grapefruit last night and then counted each one." Ellen then asked, "Well, how can we get an answer if you don't know?" Ms Thompson emphatically responded, "The answer is within your power to know. Do you think all problems have answers provided?"

Students began to work in their groups. One group measured Alex, a member of the group, and then estimated how many Alexes tall the room was. They told Alex to lie down and they measured the length and width of the room. They began to argue among themselves about how many grapefruit would make the length of Alex. Finally, they agreed Alex was 17 grapefruits long.

Another group looked at the ceiling tiles and counted them. There were 33 tiles across and 40 tiles long. John said that 33 times 10 was 330 and then he kept adding: 330, 660, 1200, 1400. Adriana shook her head and said, "No, 660 and 660 is not 1200. It is more than that. 600 and 600 is 1200. You have to add the extra 60s." John took out a pencil and began to write 60 plus 60 = 120. He tried writing 1200 + 120 and paused for a minute.

Argha responded with, "Let me have the pencil." He wrote 1000 + 200 + 120 + 1320. The group appeared satisfied and continued to think about the grapefruits. Adriana asked the group, "How does the number of tiles help us figure out how many grapefruit? All we know is how many tiles on the ceiling." John appeared to be losing patience. "How many grapefruits do you think will fit in each tile?" Adriana sat and looked at the ceiling and after a few minutes said, "Fifteen."

Ms. Thompson walked over to another group. The students were staring at the teacher's closet.

Jessica: I think 55 grapefruit will fill the front of the closet and about 7 rows of grapefruit in.
Meryl: How many is that?
Jessica: I don't know.
Meryl: Kim, how many?
Kim: Get the calculator.
Jessica: 385 grapefruit.
Meryl: I think there are enough spaces for 10 closets along this wall.
Kim: Then there would be 15 closets on this wall because it's bigger.

Jessica tells the group to wait a minute and she computes using the calculator again.

Jessica: 150.
Meryl: We didn't think about the 385 grapefruit. Now what do we do?
Jessica: Add 385 to 150.
Kim: No. We multiply. There are 385 grapefruit in every closet and there can be 150 closets.

FOUR TYPES OF CLASSROOM QUESTIONS

My preference in the classroom is for questions and learning to be situated in student interest and curiosity. Given the reality and accountability of schools today, this may seem unrealistic. How to find the right mix of classroom questioning deserves attention here.

I have delineated four types of classroom questions:

1. Verbal worksheets—these are teacher-initiated questions to which there are answers that are "known and correct."

2. Problem-solving questions—these are often simple questions requiring complex solutions.

[margin handwritten notes: think about... I've been engaged, learning, fun... Think of classes when... students in your? how engage all]

3. Teachable moment questions—these are usually student-generated and emerge from student curiosity or need to know.

4. Information-driven questions—these are either student or teacher questions stemming from basic information needs.

Whether you are teaching social studies, language arts, or mathematics, most questions fall into the categories of verbal worksheets and information-driven questions. This is in part, due to the way in which we test children with multiple choice, single answer questions, and a lower-level recall of information. It is a more expedient and quicker assessment to ask students if they know the material covered in the same way in which the content was taught. It requires more reflection and thinking on the part of the teacher and the learner to engage in questions that call for application of knowledge learned or thinking about what has been learned in different ways. Classrooms in which the mix of questions are of the nature of problem-solving and teachable moment questions expect learning to extend beyond facts and recall and ask children to think, analyze, posit, wonder, and synthesize.

✖ CLASSROOM QUESTIONS

Type of Question	Who Asks?	Thinking Required	Who Answers?	Example
Verbal worksheet	Teacher	Low	One with the right answer	"What is a four-sided figure with only two parallel sides called?"
Problem-solving	Teacher or student	High	Individual or groups of children	"How many grapefruit will fit in this room?"
Teachable moment	Curious student	High	Other students, teacher, students themselves, or resources in and out of school community	"Why are boys not allowed to wear hats, but girls can?"
Information-driven	Teacher or student	Low to medium	Teacher, student, or school community personnel	"What time are parent conferences?"

word talk?

The key in classroom questioning is to require thinking—for questions to demand cognitive engagement that require more than simple, already established solution pathways such as plugging numbers into a formula where the level of thinking needed is limited to determining which formula to use. Questions may be posed by the teacher and still elevate thinking to a level where students themselves are generating new questions to think about in order to find a solution to the original question posed.

The grapefruit question is an example of this kind of extended questioning that results from the original query. Possible additional student-generated questions that might surface in the solution process are:

What size are the grapefruit? What if there are different sizes?

Do we include the classroom furniture in our solution?

What about the spaces between the grapefruit? Do we account for them?

What if we squish the grapefruit? Sometimes you can do this. Or squeeze them.

Learning in this way builds capacity to see the world as multidimensional and complex, because there is no known answer and no quick response expected. It is impossible to see a flurry of student hands being rapidly raised, eager to show the teacher and classmates how "smart" they are—but rather a classroom behavior that necessitates students to "think before you respond." Who can deny we need more of that in our world?

Typical classroom dialogue is often limited to a pattern of the teacher asking verbal worksheet questions to which the answers are known or where there are generally acceptable "known" answers. Questions of this sort might be used to determine if students are paying attention or as a means for the teacher to find out who can recall the material just covered. It has only been in recent years that classroom discourse has been studied in relation to practice that is socially constructed. A more open-ended pattern of questioning, often originating with a student question and leading to student-to-student dialogue, allows for students to put forth their own ideas and thinking in the process of developing understanding (Cazden, 2001; Wells, 1993).

Research on students working in groups to discuss and solve problems with a teacher's occasional guidance has origins as early as Dewey (1938/1963) and Vygotsky (1978) and as recently as O'Neill and Polman (2004). It behooves us as educators to be mindful of how we ask questions, the nature of those questions, and how we plan and allow for students to take an active role in shaping the dialogue around their own, as well as teacher-initiated, questions. Nowhere is this more eloquently explained than in the following story told by Angelo Ciardiello (1998) in an article titled "Did You Ask a Good Question Today?" The mother of the future Nobel laureate in physics always asked her son on his return home after school each day, "Did you ask a good question today?" Rabi, her son, credits this ability to ask good questions as the motivating force in his becoming a scientist as this runs counter to typical classroom behavior where the teacher asks the questions and the students are expected to answer them with the "correct" answers.

As simple as it may seem to expect students to ask questions as well as answer them, students receive minimal opportunities to ask hypothesis-generating questions in classrooms. Questions requiring a higher level of cognitive demand stimulate divergent thinking and lead to a new appreciation of learning since the reward for gaining knowledge in these instances is self-gratifying rather than "teacher-pleasing." The following two vignettes are examples of learning resulting from students' own need to know.

WHEN THE QUEST TO KNOW ← COMES FROM WITHIN

Students in an elementary school in Manhattan asked their teacher why kids fight so much at their school. Mrs. Anderson saw the students' question as the perfect chance to launch a new math learning project. She envisioned the question as a means for students to problem solve and to connect learning to their own interests and concerns. She jump-started the project by asking the students how they might go about finding an answer to the question. Students said they could survey the kids in the school. Mrs. Anderson told them to form a group to work on the questions for the survey. She asked what would be other ways they could gather information that might help them think about the question. Students responded with suggestions for people they might interview—the principal, teachers, and the secretary, since she knows everything that happens in the school. For the next several weeks students were actively engaged in creating a survey and analyzing the data results, interviewing several school personnel and listening to the taped interviews several times, and making graphs to represent the survey data. Here is the report written by the students:

We are in New York City at a school in Manhattan. We study different things in our neighborhood that we want to know about. This year, we wanted to know why kids fight in our school. It is a problem for us. We don't want kids to fight because they could get injured or hurt.

We did surveys and interviews in our school to help us answer our question. We interviewed three teachers, the principal, the assistant principal, and secretary. We surveyed about 125 students in grades 3 to 5. We thought doing surveys and interviews of these people would help us understand why kids fight.

Survey Results:

We asked about 125 students at our school four different questions. When all of our data were collected we tallied the responses and created graphs to show what we learned. Please take a moment to look at our graphs.

Question #1: Have you ever encouraged a fight?
    Yes = 29
    No = 95
Question #2: Why do you think students fight?
    Someone does something to you first = 47
    Not sharing = 12
    Bullying = 38
    Gossiping = 13
Question #3: Is fighting a problem in school?
    Yes = 92
    No = 22
Question #4: Have you ever been in a fight?
    Yes = 64
    No = 65

What we learned from the interviews:

When we interviewed the teachers about why they thought kids in our school fight they said that students get into fights for a lot of different reasons. They are that students get frustrated when they don't get their own way, or they just want attention, they think they are tough, or they try to defend themselves. Teachers also said that students fight for no reason at all.

Teachers said they try to prevent fights in many ways. Some encourage their students to work out their problems. Other teachers separate their kids from fights. The teachers mostly try to prevent fights before they happen.

We interviewed our school secretary and found out something amazing. She said she thought that kids fight more today than in the past. We think this might be because students were physically punished for misbehaving. Today, kids don't seem to care. They know that they will have some sort of punishment, but it won't be physical.

What we discovered:

This study has shown us that fighting is a problem in our school. It's happening in classrooms and in the yard. One major reason we think it's happening is because kids want attention. Here are the results of our survey about fighting in school:

Is Fighting a Problem in School?

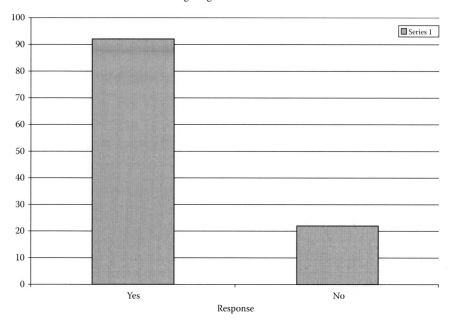

Have You Ever Been in a Fight?

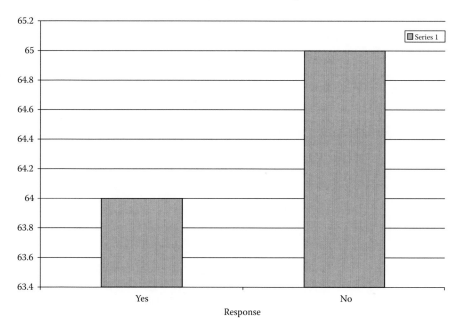

Have You Ever Encouraged a Fight?

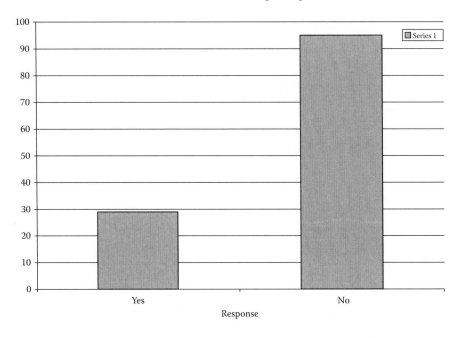

Why Do You Think Students Fight?

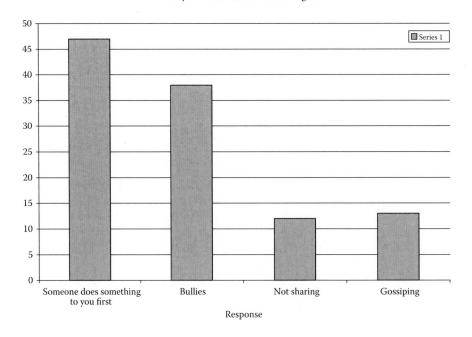

Students continued their interest in the "fighting dilemma" by focusing on the prevention aspect. They approached the school principal with a plan to have student playground monitors who would oversee playground games and provide an unbiased intervention in cases of game rule confusion. They requested "Playground Monitor" T-shirts from the principal and worked out a monthly monitor recess schedule. Nowhere is a sense of purpose more explicit than meeting a real life problem, such as the why kids fight dilemma, and finding a solution that addresses the immediate needs of all participants. In doing so resiliency is nurtured through the building of social competency, cultivating problem-solving skills and group decision making, while providing students with a sense of purpose.

NCTM's five process standards were addressed in this investigation. Embedded in this study were the process standards of problem solving, reasoning and proof, communication, connections, and representation. These processes reflect the manner in which mathematics is learned and how students acquire and use knowledge. The Park Study project described in the section that follows and the Why Kids Fight project depict student learning motivated by a single question to understand a phenomenon students experienced in their lives, at their own school. In the following account of the Park Study by Mrs. Anderson, the teacher of the children who asked the question, take note of the way in which she guides their inquiry.

Park Study

My students showed a natural curiosity in the neighborhood parks. On the first day that we were together, I asked them what they were interested in learning. Immediately, one student responded that they wanted to go outside. I was not familiar with the area, so I had them lead me to the nearest park. The students played a variety of games with numerous rules and exhausted themselves by the time that we had to leave. I asked the children the same question the next day, and again they responded that they wanted to go to the park. However, this time they wanted to go to the "good" park even though it was farther away. So we went. This pattern continued until we had visited five parks in the community. At the end of our "park tour" I asked, "Which park is the best?" Immediately, all five names were shouted and debated. I asked the students to justify their opinions and they set off in groups to chart the different characteristics of the parks. After creating a cluttered assortment of responses such as "Kelley Park doesn't have swings"; "Chelsea Park has a basketball court"; and "Seal Park is just for little kids," the students organized their work into a table showing each park with the appropriate number of boxes checked. The students sat back to admire the work they had just done.

how practically?

It was then that I asked, "So, what else do you want to know that this table doesn't tell you?"

One child asked, "Which park do more people go to?"

Another asked, "When do most people go to the park?"

"How could we answer these questions?"

The students offered many ideas. Some thought that we could survey community members and other students in the school. Others thought it would be better if we actually went to the parks to do observations. I felt the excitement growing in the classroom that day as the students started putting together their own investigation into something that they were curious about.

As evident from these two examples, student questioning was the focal point for the learning that occurred. Student questioning generated from student wonderment that calls for prediction, thoughtful experimenting, discussion, and application is what characterizes a higher level of cognitive thought that is essential to the problem-solving process. Helping students to generate thought-provoking questions that result in a search for knowledge and understanding is a difficult challenge. According to White and Gunstone (1992), teachers' first attempts at getting students to ask questions about what they want to know and that require a processing of ideas failed. Students' questions were largely found to be purely factual, closed questions. When teachers want to control the questioning the result is more passive student responses. When students ask questions that require knowledge the questions often arise from student interest in making sense of their world that is distinctly different from questions rooted in the text where a need to know is related to recall of information.

Research shows that giving students more input into the learning process improves student efficacy (Heron, 2003). Heron reports in her study of classroom culture and teacher–student relationships that teachers need to trust students and allow them time for discussions about complex issues that matter. This promotes a curiosity for learning that is a powerful learning motivator. Self-questioning is a potent cognitive strategy for helping students to learn mathematics content and processes because coming up with their own questions prompts learners to search for answers that they are interested in knowing (Rosenshine, Meister, & Chapman, 1996).

COVERING THE CURRICULUM

It is the common cry of teachers that they do not have enough time to deviate from the curriculum with the increased pressure on them to prepare students for passing city and state tests. Fear of not introducing and teaching specified content areas is what keeps many educators from allowing student interest and questions to motivate learning. I felt the same pressure as a fourth-grade teacher when I was team teaching and not using the prescribed curriculum for our daily instruction structure. Every year we feared that our students might do poorly on the tests and therefore put them at a disadvantage. It took a few years of waiting for test results to return and seeing our students performing as well, or better, than any other fourth-grade class in our school for us to relax and trust in our instructional approach to learning. That is what it takes, *trust* and a belief that you are providing your students with more learning rather than thinking in terms of a deficit.

If we examine closely both the Why Kids Fight Study and the Park Study we find the following content standards from the *Principles and Standards for School Mathematics* (NCTM) introduced or addressed in these projects:

Algebra

- Understand patterns, relations, and functions
- Use mathematical models to represent and understand quantitative relationships
- Analyze change in various contexts

Measurement

- Apply appropriate techniques, tools, and formulas to determine measurements

Data Analysis and Probability

- Formulate questions that can be addressed with data and collect, organize, and display relevant data to answer them
- Select and use appropriate statistical methods to analyze data
- Develop and evaluate inferences and predictions that are based on data
- Understand and apply basic concepts of probability

Once you dissect project learning and realize that content is being covered it becomes easier to justify letting children's curiosity and wonderment guide some of the learning in the classroom. The mere fact that the work students are doing is project based does not mean mathematical content is not being covered. As teachers, understanding where and how content is embedded in any assignment is critical for your sense of accountability. It is also important to be clear about the mathematics children are learning when you articulate to colleagues and administrators how you are teaching core curriculum content.

A WHOLE SCHOOL APPROACH
TO ASKING QUESTIONS

The discussion thus far has centered on classroom questions because that is where many student queries happen. I included the following example of a whole school run by students, where student ideas and thinking are the engine of the school machinery. I heard Richard Gerver address an audience of educators from around the world about his school at a UNESCO world conference on integrated education in Lisbon, Portugal, in April 2006. Mr. Gerver is headmaster of the Grangeton Primary School in England and he changed the ethos of school and learning for the 430 children, ranging in age from 3 to 11, who attend the school. Until Gerver was hired as head teacher, Grangeton was considered one of the worst primary schools in the United Kingdom.

As the new headmaster Gerver used critical questions to motivate his work. "Why do our children not want to go to school as much as they want to go to Disneyland?" "What do we want these students to be as human beings?" Children have to recognize that learning is important to them. The school experience cannot be focused on, "You'll get a good job if you get good grades." Gerver believed we must get better at marketing the idea of learning to children.

At Grangeton, Gerver explained that life skills are what they are teaching: working in teams, the positivity of risk taking, and the importance of making mistakes and failing. He described the result of such a focus as excitement, engagement, questioning, and aspiration. In the Grangeton Project, the children run the school. They have a mayor who is elected by the students. Gerver told the audience that that year's mayor was 10 years old and even as the head teacher, he himself had to answer to the mayor. He went on to explain that there is a national curriculum that he must adhere to. He chose to address the curriculum in a creative fashion by creating an environment of empowerment and student inquiry.

The school is a series of centers that provides for the community. The children run these centers and fund their own work. For those skeptics who believe such an initiative doesn't embody the scholarly rigor of more traditional school experiences, Gerver shared the following data to provide evidence to the contrary. Within 18 months, Grangeton's test scores had doubled on the state exams. The following comments from students at Grangeton highlight the way in which the learning experience has been transformed for students: "I love my school," " My school is special," and "I make my school special."

Gerver also believes that U.K. teacher training programs are too prescriptive and operate out of a culture of fear. As a result they create teachers who operate within a culture of fear. He intentionally chose to give his teachers permission to be creative and to cultivate student self-motivation. He encouraged them to be innovative and to listen to student questions and needs, which in turn fostered creativity in children.

At the same conference another inspirational speaker, Sir Ken Robinson, author of *Out of Our Minds* (2001), believes systems of public education throughout the world are too focused on raising standards of literacy and numeracy by standardization of curricula. He believes that by directing learning in this way we are inadequately meeting the challenges of our global economies and cultures. According to him, a sounder approach is to center learning on diversity, complexity, student autonomy, and uncertainty. He has advised governments in Europe, Asia, and the United States, as well as Fortune 500 companies on the need for creativity and for a student's questions and perseverance in seeking answers to be considered part of academic ability. "We are currently educating our children from the neck up, and slightly to one side. ... Our future is in the power of our imagination" (Robinson, 2006).

LEARNING THROUGH DIALOGUE:
LAURA'S NEED TO KNOW

Laura, a graduate student who approached me about doing an independent study on student math discourse, was interested in understanding why the students in the classroom where she was doing her student teaching would write about their math thinking but rarely share their ideas orally. I present here portions of her research, her quest to understand, and what she learned. This is a two-layered student-driven study—about Laura's motivation to know and how she let her questions drive her learning, as well as about the students she was studying and how their questions and ideas blossomed.

Farmer Brown Had a Farm, Eei Eei Oo

In the heart of New York City, on the upper east side of Manhattan, there lives a class of 26 fourth-grade students. Overlooking the busy New York streets, 26 desks are in six groups of four or five desks each, which are arranged in a classroom just big enough to hold room for a large rug area. The room is decorated with reading and writing strategies, math concepts, or social studies projects. The fourth graders, each unique in race, culture, and personality, work day in and day out on hands-on activities.

NCTM communication standards ask the teacher to orchestrate discourse by: posing tasks that engage and challenge students' thinking; deciding when to let a student struggle or when to clarify an issue; and also asking students to clarify their findings orally and in writing. I wanted to follow these standards, so I gave my students the following problem that would challenge their thinking: "One day Farmer Brown was counting her pigs and chickens. She noticed that they had 60 legs and that there were 22 animals in all. How many of each kind of animal (pigs and chickens) did she have?" I asked them to work in their assigned pairs where they were to write down their mathematical work and solutions, record the processes of their work, and orally present their findings to the class.

The results to this two-part lesson were truly fascinating. The first day the students were given a little less than an hour to work on the problem with their partner. Right away I heard, "it's impossible," "I don't get it," and "I can't do it." The problem challenged them so much that they wanted to give up right away, but I would not allow that to occur. In response I would say, "It's not impossible, you can do it, and just keep trying." At the beginning, I saw many pairs struggle with the idea of dividing 22 by 2 and 60 by 2 because 2 is the total number of different animals. The students thought that the answers to 60 divided by 2 and 22 divided by 2 were their final answers. I had to explain to them that if you divide 60 legs by 2 animals you would have forgotten about the heads. Once it was established that they really needed to think about using all the numbers together in some sort of format, the students started to analyze and reflect. Students worked throughout the period using a process of elimination (guess and check) or collaborating with their peers to find solutions.

The following day each pair had to orally explain the solutions and strategies. I videotaped this segment. I did not ask many questions during the presentation, as I wanted the other classmates to do the probing. It is suggested by NCTM that teachers do more listening and the student do the reasoning. I wanted to see if the students could orally support themselves and if their peers could analyze the thinking process. A pair of students went up in front of the class and talked about their answers. "We got 14 chickens and 8 pigs for our answer. We got this because 8 pigs times 4 gives us 32, and 14 chickens times 2 gives us 28. So 8 plus 14 gives us 22 animals, and 32 plus 28 gives us 60 legs." A student asked, "Where did you get the 4 and 2?" The pair answered, "The 4 and 2 are the number of legs for each animal." Then silence. I would ask, "Any more questions for this group?" No hands.

The next pair would start the same process over. I had about three or four students, out of 26, discuss their strategy of using a chart or pictures to figure out their answer. Why were the groups not talking about their processes? I know most students started with 22 divided by 2; why did they not mention this? Why was no one else asking these questions? These questions lingered in my mind that afternoon after our session together.

The following day I sat down with my university professor and the other two members of my independent math study group to discuss my findings. I showed them student work and the videotape of the students. Together we came up with some findings about the lesson and the students.

By comparing what students wrote in their notebooks and what they orally presented to their classmates, we found the two types of information to be completely different.

Let's Reflect

Joan, for example, had explanations, mathematical work, and charts in her written work, but she only mentioned to the class her strategy of using a chart. Here is some excerpts from her written work. "I made 6 circles. I put tally marks in the circles to represent pigs and chickens, 2 legs for chickens and 4 for pigs. I put 10 tally marks in each circle since I know that $6 \times 10 = 60$. Once I had that done, all I needed to do was count the pigs and chickens to see if there were 22 animals in all." When she orally participated, this was how she explained her chart, "I used tally marks to represent pigs and chickens, 2 for chickens and 4 for pigs." I asked, "What does the 2 and 4 represent?" She answered, "They are the number of legs. I put 10 of them in 6 different circles." One student interrupts to ask, "Where did you get the 10 from?" "I used 10 because $10 \times 6 = 60$. I know there had to be 22 animals in all so the answer came out to be 8 pigs and 14 chickens." The difference between her written response and her oral presentation was in the detail of her explanations and clarification of what the numbers represented. There was more support, justification, and reflection in her written ~ ? work than in her presentation.

Alan provided another example of how the written work was stronger ? number than the oral presentation. His written work explains, "First I had to multiply and try which two numbers multiplied by 4 or 2, the number of legs, would give me 60 legs and 22 heads." His work shows how he tried $16 \times 4 = 64$ and $12 \times 2 = 24$ or $6 \times 4 = 24$ and $20 \times 2 = 40$. After his work he wrote, "Those answers, when you add them together, you will get 60." It is clear through analyzing his work that Alan tried to first find which two numbers equaled 60 legs total. When Alan came up to present, he automatically said, "We got 14 chickens and 8 pigs, etc., etc.," just like the response of many of his other classmates. He was not supporting his work in the oral presentation the way that he had done in the written response.

When reflecting on the results of the Farmer Brown problem questions rose to my mind. I had questions about why the lesson and the end results happened the way they did. I started to research articles about discourse in the classroom and strategies to facilitate communication. Since the Farmer Brown problem was shared in a larger group setting, and worked on in pairs, I wanted to find a different way to work on and share story problems that would hopefully increase communication support to the level that the fourth graders' writing ability was on.

Large Group to Small Group

Through my research I wanted to find articles that taught me strategies that would encourage communication in the classroom. Three articles show two separate ideas of how classrooms can promote communication. Greenes and Schulman (1996) understand that communication not only helps clarification and understanding of students' thinking, but it also helps to reveal what students know and do not know and their reasoning. The authors use two types of exploration to promote communication: short term and long term. Short-term explorations are done in class either individually or with a partner. These activities contain all the necessary data to solve the problem. The students make their observations, in a chart or using pictures, and document their solutions in their notebooks. They would then discuss to receive feedback (Greenes & Schulman, 1996). The long-term exploration uses more investigations and prior knowledge to finding an answer. Students collect data, organize and analyze it, and then present the data and the findings. These are done over a period of time as a collective group (Greenes & Schulman, 1996).

The other two articles look at problem solving in collaborative groups. To compare this idea to the last article, the two authors looked at how small groups work on long-term explorations. Communication is essential for small-group experience, but that experience needs to be structured to maximize the chance of communication (Artzt, 1996). Just like with the challenge of discourse in the classroom, group members must feel happy in their group and have appropriate social skills for interaction to occur.

Artzt (1996) and Tanner and Casados (1998) talk in their research articles about guidelines that they use in their small-group activities. Artzt categorizes the behaviors of the students in small groups to evaluate the reasoning that the students are doing. The four categories are talking about the problem, doing the problem, watching or listening, and off task. Artzt believes that once students become aware of the role of such problem-solving behaviors, they can begin to use them in their individual work. Once he assesses the students' behaviors in a problem-solving situation, he is able to see which students took a more passive role, which students were off task, or which students dominated the discussion. He can then take measures to change the make up of a small group or assign different roles to the students. In the end, students will be able to engage in mathematical reasoning more easily.

Michael Tanner and Leah Casados looked at small groups as well, but more closely at the guidelines for students and teachers. Casados followed the method of Socratic seminars to help promote classroom discussion. Some of the guidelines that she followed in her problem-solving lesson were to listen to one another, focus on math content, use a time limit of

30 minutes, begin a discussion with a question, and end a discussion with a summary statement. After using her guidelines in the classroom discussions on math concepts, Casados recognized that her students were becoming more insightful through taking ownership of their ideas. She says, "The more I used discussions, the more I enjoyed watching the students bounce ideas off each other and use logic to solve problems, and I also can spot problems and misconceptions in student understanding just by listening." The main idea behind the work of these researchers is that there needs to be some kind of structure in small-group work. Whether it is analyzing student behaviors or giving students guidelines for discussion, it is the importance of communication in math that will spark the children to speak.

Moving from Farms to Stairs

I decided to take the ideas from these research studies and structure the next problem-solving activity in my fourth-grade class. I put the fourth graders into small groups and gave them another challenging problem. I observed the interactions between the students while they solved the problem. The problem read: "Alexis, Hamilton, and Dallas were at the bottom of a staircase. That was their only way out of a mineshaft. They could leave only by going out one at a time and thought that their best plan was not to step on the same steps on the way out. After a short consultation, they made a plan: each person would step with his or her left foot on the first step. After that, Alexis would walk the steps one at a time, alternating feet as usual, but Hamilton would skip one step and Dallas would skip two steps on their way out. They wondered a few questions: On which step from the bottom would their right feet first land? On which step would all three people land? If the staircase had 191 steps, what would be the last step on which all three people would land? Land with their left feet? Land with their right feet?"

The group started by assigning their own roles—two secretaries, a leader, and a facilitator—because they felt it was the best idea. I did not tell the group to assign roles, but I think it is important to make sure everyone is involved. The group had a great deal of trouble starting because all four members were on a "different page." Joan, the leader, understood the problem too fast for Kari and Fran, who were completely lost, and Alejandro was just trying to calm everyone down. They decided to start all over again. They wrote down the general information about how each person climbed the steps. They then decided to go to the staircase in the school to help them figure out the problem. What really opened everyone's eyes to the problem was using the school staircase as a resource. Three of them each acted out a different person's role climbing the stairs, while the fourth recorded which feet landed on which steps. The last question was the hardest to figure out for them. Joan took the lead and delegated each student to write out the pattern of steps each person would land on. For example, Alan wrote the pattern out for Hamilton, and Kari wrote the pattern out for Dallas. Together the four of them found the similar numbers between each person and made a decision as to the answer for the last step that Alexis, Hamilton, and Dallas would all land on.

It was interesting to watch the behaviors, as mentioned by Artzt, which each student had in the group. Joan was more dominant compared to Fran, who was more passive. This exercise proved to me that small-group work probed much more oral communication by the group members. Ironically, when I collected the work by the team, not much was written down. Joan had started a chart to organize her thoughts but never finished. Alan had his pattern of footsteps written down, but nothing to explain what the meanings of the numbers were, and Kari, the secretary, gave up writing when the problem became difficult for her. They were so involved in determining the answer and vocalizing their justifications for their findings that they neglected the written part. I know this has something to do with using the staircase as a resource. Their involvement in solving the problem by using the stairs overshadowed writing down any of their words. The stairs were a great resource but drew their attention away from writing.

Kari is a great example of a student who is stronger in her oral participation than in her written work. She was labeled the secretary; her job was to have written everything that was going on in the group. When the problem became a challenge for Kari, she put her clipboard down and stopped writing. Notice how Kari writes about the introductory ideas, like Dallas skips two steps and Hamilton skips one, and then jumps from there to a number pattern. The pattern is counting by 3's, but nowhere has Kari written what the pattern represents or why she wrote it. Yet by looking at the observation notes, the reader can see that Joan had asked Kari to write the number pattern for Dallas, starting at the number seven. This was because they wanted to see which step was similar between each character.

Fran solved the problem in the same way that Kari had. Fran's written work starts off strong with all the introductory material laid out, but then, like Kari, she stops. Her work shows some kind of division she did between 191 and 7 but no explanation as to why she did that. The observation notes help justify her work. The group was trying to figure out the last question of the problem: "What would be the last step that all three characters would land on if the staircase was 191 steps high?" They knew from an earlier answer that the first step they all land on is the seventh step and so Fran voiced to the group, "Hey let's divide 191 into 7 to see what is the similar step." She was able to orally tell her group her thinking process but not able to explain in her written response. It seems clear by analyzing the work and the criteria chart that the four students neglected the written part of the exercise and focused all their attention on vocalizing their explanations.

Implications in the Classroom

To continue my study on classroom discourse in mathematics, I kept following this notion of small-group work. I would try short-term and long-term explorations, assign roles and guidelines, and even try to assess student behaviors. There are many more ways to promote an even balance between expressing ideas orally and in writing. I hoped to find just the right routine that would fit my class so that students would have strength in writing and vocalizing their mathematical findings and justifications.

In the past, classroom discussion usually meant just going over answers from the homework or fixing the mistakes. It was much more teacher centered than student driven (Tanner & Casados, 1998). Today, discussion means much more in mathematics and in the classroom. NCTM principles and standards for mathematics state that students "be able to reflect upon and clarify their thinking about mathematical ideas and relationships, and express mathematical ideas orally and in writing" (Tanner & Casados, 1998). The idea of discourse in the math environment has been emphasized a great deal recently. I have seen it through the emphasis on written responses and oral explanations in fourth grade. Probing students with "whys" or asking them to explain is a great way for interaction to happen. A teacher has the responsibility to enhance the interaction between students, encourage them to question one another, and create a respectful, open environment.

I have been student teaching this academic year in the New York City public schools. In such a diverse urban city as New York, there can be many problems that arise in the classroom. I have seen the students get so involved in a mathematical discussion that hands start flying up in the air and multiple views are voiced. This happens because the environment that these students gather in each day is open and free to views and discussion on mathematics and other such topics. Discourse is a word that students may not know or understand, but they all participate in it.

One of the most incredible learning experiences of my career happened when I was approached by three graduate students each yearning to gain deeper understandings about a particular issue regarding mathematics teaching and learning. Each of these students came to me independent of the others and asked if I would be willing to do an independent study with them. I suggested to Anthony, Laura, and Meg that all four of us enter into a shared learning experience. Although they each had specific wonderings that were driving them to learn more, there was a great deal of overlap among their questions. Anthony was interested in math journals, Laura wanted to explore the ways in which students expressed their mathematical thinking, and Meg was curious about the classroom environment and its impact on individual students. What occurred during this semester was extraordinary. As we put our thinking and ideas into the air for critique and application by the group, we all became enriched. The letter below is Anthony's letter to me at the end of this learning involvement that led each of us to a new professional learning awareness.

Dear Judy,

When I consider what my ideal classroom environment would be like, I think of an array of characteristics. I think of a class where students are excited to come in and even more excited when they leave. A place where the content is rooted in the students' interests and where the learning is done between the students, not to them. It's a place where the quest for knowledge is contagious as students feed off and motivate each other to keep taking their efforts to a new level. Students have just as much interest in the work of their peers as their own, and use that to help their studies. It's a place where students explore the unknown and take risks in their learning because the environment makes them feel comfortable doing so. Most of all, it's a place, when being described, in which the teacher isn't mentioned once—because he or she has become a student as well. However, it will always be remembered as a group environment fostered by that teacher.

What's great about these characteristics is that they have helped shape my philosophy of teaching and learning, and through our independent study together, our setting has provided a model for what learning can truly be. This is certainly a model that I think can generalize to any classroom at any level. Our focus happened to be on math, but what was interesting to see was our common objectives explored in such different ways. I think we would agree that we set out to become better math teachers, but more specifically, explore some questions. What is student understanding of math? How do you capture it? How is it communicated? What environment is best for doing that learning? What are the important elements of that environment? In all, how can we become the best math teachers we can be? Our answer is by learning math ourselves, exploring it through our students, and supporting each other.

My research and learning was manifested through the math journal. While Meg focused more on individual students and the environment, Laura seemed to bridge our areas by focusing on communication and discussion in the math classroom. We drew similar conclusions to the same questions, however, and learned from each other's work and experiences.

At the heart of all this learning was the environment established by the teacher. Although the students carry the success of the class with their work and efforts, it is created and facilitated by an outstanding teacher. The teacher realizes that the best learning lies in a student that is constantly assessing his or her own learning. As Ron Berger said in his book, the most valuable assessment is not done to the students, it's the assessment done inside the students. When an environment is created in which we could explore our own questions, we are motivated to take risks and monitor the quality of our learning ourselves.

I hope you don't take this personally, Judy, because the setting and the guidance you offered was invaluable. But I learned more about what kind of environment I want my classroom to be from us together, especially from Meg, than anywhere else. I have learned more about sharing math and oral communication than anywhere else because of our collective efforts, and especially from Laura. And above all, I have learned so much from you, Judy, but what you have taught me most is what you did know and allowed me to discover on my own.

 Good teachers inspire their students, as you have us. However, great teachers are inspired by their students as well, which is also what you make us feel. You made our projects seem purposeful, important, and valuable. Seeing your excitement in our work only made us more motivated to do more. I now have an unimagined passion for teaching math. Only a few months ago I considered it one of my weakest domains, and now I consider it one of my most valuable assets in my "teaching arsenal."

In the end, it wouldn't have happened without the setting and the environment created by you and us together. We had the chance to create a small and intimate learning circle to explore our common ideas together. Although our explorations had different makeups, we synthesized our findings and thoughts. On top of it all, our sessions only got better and more in-depth, even to the point where we find ourselves leaving each meeting with new questions and an eagerness to jump back in the pool.

On a broader note, I thank each of us involved. Laura, Meg, and yourself, each made me a better math teacher and a better teacher because of our experience. It taught me a lot about how being a teacher is being a scholar as well, and I think that we really brought out the best in each other. More specifically, I thank you, Judy, for making this real. It was amazing and I can't really put how this experience has made me feel in words. Teaching is my passion and I am now better at it because of this experience and because of you. Thanks for everything.

Anthony

TEACHER AS RESEARCHER THOUGHTS

1. Keep a tally record of the types of questions students ask in a day. What does your recording of questions tell you?

	Open	*Closed*
Beginning of day as children arrive	IIII	I
Math	II	IIII
Literacy	II	II
Science	IIIII IIIII II	I
Transitions between classes	II	IIII
End of day	IIII IIII	III

hmm

2. Keep a record of issues and questions students talk about at recess. How might student interest lead to a learning project in your classroom?

3. Keep a large class chart with a list of questions students ask. Use this to frame an end-of-the-year investigation that is chosen by students.

Chapter 4

How Can I Tune Transitions to a New Key?

"It is now 9:49. Let's see if it is possible for us to clean up our desks, put away all materials, and gather on the rug for a discussion in 15 minutes or less."

This is the message Carol and I posted on the overhead for our fourth-grade students. The students had spent the morning working in groups on creating travel brochures for a unit on *Trumpet of the Swan* by E. B. White. The classroom was a hodgepodge: paper of all colors, textures, and sizes spread out on student desks; paste and scissors strewn about; resource books everywhere; paint, crayons, markers, and even glitter on desktops and students. We did not mention the overhead message—just positioned it on the overhead in clear view. Within minutes, a few students noticed the message and the communication spread throughout the classroom. Students glanced up at the clock and immediately began to tidy up their spaces. Children were busy sorting paper, returning scissors to a basket, and scrambling to the bathroom to wash the glitter and glue from their hands and gather dampened paper towels to wash the desktops. By 10:12 everyone was seated on the rug in the meeting corner of the classroom.

"Did we make it in 15 minutes?" Carol asked the class.

"Yes, it isn't 15 minutes past 10 yet."

Carol waited.

"But we started before 10," someone called out.

"It took us 11 minutes plus 12 minutes," someone replied. "We took longer than 15 minutes."

"How many minutes over were we?" I asked.

"Well, if you add the 11 and 12 you get 23. 23 take away 15 is, um, I don't know."

"Add 3 to the 12 and take away the 3 from the 11. We were 8 minutes over. Does everyone agree?"

Students nod in agreement.

"What could we do more efficiently next time to make it in 15 minutes?"

The mathematics being learned here is real life, everyday problem solving. How many times in a day do we encounter this kind of dilemma? I need to be at the doctor's by 3:00 and it usually takes me 40 to 50 minutes if the traffic isn't bad. If there is unusually bad weather or an accident, I should allow an even longer amount of time to arrive promptly at my appointment. What time must I leave home to get there in time? Or, if I take the express train to Brooklyn, I can make the trip to Park Slope in 25 minutes, but the express only leaves from Chambers Street Station and I will need to change trains. Will it be faster to take the local and not have to make a change?

The overhead message we posted provides students with an opportunity to solve problems within a real-life context. It is motivating for them to take responsibility for the problem and try to better their own efficiency in the process. This strategy might not provide the same level of stimulus if used frequently, but as an infrequent tactic it can be unparalleled for getting students to shift from one activity to another with a minimum of chaos and confusion. The challenge for us as teachers is to devise a variety of methods for transitioning from one learning endeavor to another. Too often, however, we function from a reactionary stance and resort to a raising of the voice, "Okay, put everything away and come to the rug" mode. Over time, students begin to tune out such requests and move at their own transitioning pace, with repeated admonitions from the teacher.

I gave my graduate students an assignment as follows:

> In your student teaching placement, document the time allocation of activity for one day. Begin recording the nature of student activity the moment school begins and end when the students are dismissed at the end of the day.

One student teacher's documentation looked like this:

Transitions

8:47–8:48	Instructions given in the hall before students enter the classroom
8:48–8:50	Students hang up their coats and unpack their backpacks; by 8:50, some students have begun on their do-now work (portfolios), but some have not *3 minutes*
8:50–9:10	Students work on portfolios
9:10–9:12	Whole class moves to the rug *2 minutes*
9:12–9:23	Morning meeting
9:23–10:09	Poetry

10:09–10:11	Students get their book baskets from the classroom library *2 minutes*
10:11–10:20	Independent reading, book club meetings (as called by the teacher)
10:18	Self-contained classroom students enter the class to wait for music
10:20–10:24	Clean up and wait for Mr. C (music teacher); at 10:23, classroom teacher suggests students read quietly while they wait *4 minutes*
10:24–10:30	Students distribute music folders; general chaos and noise *6 minutes*
10:30–11:25	Music (I left the classroom); Mr. C brings the students to music
11:25–11:29	Students walk from music to the classroom *4 minutes*
11:29–11:30	Instructions given for quiet-time work
11:30–11:53	Quiet time (finish portfolios, work on book club assignments, or other quiet activities)
11:53–11:58	Get jackets and lunches and get in line *5 minutes*
11:58–12:55	Lunch and recess
12:55–1:01	Walk from playground to classroom *6 minutes*
1:01–1:15	Enter room, unpack, quiet time *14 minutes*
1:15–1:17	Clean up, get in line to go down to reading buddies *2 minutes*
1:17–1:19	Walk down to first-grade reading buddies *4 minutes*
1:19–1:23	Waiting to enter first-grade classroom, then entering the classroom and settling on the rug *4 minutes*
1:23–1:40	Mini-lesson instructions—drawing favorite part from yesterday's field trip
1:40–1:44	Handing out materials and students finding a place to work *4 minutes*
1:44–2:10	Drawing and writing
2:10–2:13	Clean up, line up *3 minutes*
2:13–2:14	Walk up to class
2:14–2:15	Settle on the rug *2 minutes*
2:15–2:45	Read aloud and discussion
2:45–2:55	Pack things and get in line *10 minutes*
2:55	Dismissal

75 minutes of transitional activity
348 minutes for the school day
22% of the day spent in transitions

I averaged the 24 transition documentations from all the student teachers. On average, students spent 85 minutes of the school day in transitions. The average school day was made up of 364 minutes. That allowed for over an hour a day for creative use of time to infuse mathematics reasoning.

Moving from one activity to another several times throughout the school day can routinely turn into a battle of control between teacher and students. If we change the transition tune from one of control to one that taps into students' imaginations and problem-solving capacities, those transitional periods can magically be transformed into rich mathematics reasoning.

TRANSITIONING INTO NEW DESK ARRANGEMENTS

As students returned from recess they were greeted by a large map on the overhead projector depicting the desk configuration of the classroom. Each desk on the overhead was labeled with the initials of one of the students. A note was attached:

> Find your initials and SILENTLY locate your new desk location. You may communicate with each other in any way except that you are not to speak aloud until ALL students are seated in their newly assigned seats.

Students excitedly began to move about the room. They were writing signs to direct students to sit near them. Some students searched for their new table partners by studying the initials and locating their partners. Together they then used the map to find their new seats. Others went directly to their newly designated seats and waited for the other table members to arrive. Within minutes everyone was sitting at a desk with a new group of table partners. The next half hour was spent in a "getting to know something about your learning group" activity. In the process of finding their seats, students learned map skills.

Prior to this lesson, students had been asked to draw maps that would direct their parents to their desks for parent open house. Much classroom discussion revolved around creating and reading maps. What makes a map easy to read? Throughout the year the teacher worked on map-building skills by having students draw maps to scale, use a key and legend to calculate distances, and insert directional points for reference. Each of these was a mini lesson, created as a transitional diversion and interspersed throughout the year.

Ka-ming Cheng, chair professor of education and senior advisor to the vice chancellor at the University of Hong Kong, and also currently visiting professor at the Harvard School of Education, speaks about the need to foster innovation, problem solving, and collaboration in schools in this postindustrial society. Of those working in the United States today, 86% do so in small companies or settings with fewer than 20 people (Cheng, 2006). Dr. Cheng continues to explain that the human activities of our work life include communicating, brainstorming, presentations, retreats, etc., all of which require a different set of skills than those being taught in schools today. If we want our children to live healthy, balanced lives and to be contributing members of society we must teach beyond data sets and formulas; we must not limit our teaching to a single discipline, but rather, "work beyond the subject" as Dr. Cheng states. By this, he means that creative thinking and collaboration are as necessary to learning mathematics as formulas and algorithms.

Infusing mathematical reasoning throughout the day in classrooms is one way to begin to change the landscape of mathematics teaching and learning. Finding pathways to promote human ingenuity and to invigorate students may bring us closer to the image of learning in which Ka-ming Cheng hopes all children will participate.

Think about the following classroom scenario:

> Students are finishing writing in their literature response journals and the teacher wants to shift the learning focus to mathematics. She approaches a group of three girls who appear to have completed the literature journal assignment.

> *Teacher:* We need to get ready for math. Can the three of you come up with a strategy for getting everyone ready for the lesson on angle measurement with as little confusion as possible?
> *Student:* How much time do we have?
> *Teacher:* Can you have everyone ready in 5 minutes?
> *Students in unison:* Sure.

> The girls huddle briefly and then go to the writing center and begin making signs. Within minutes each girl is headed toward a different area of the classroom. Sasha stands on a chair and begins singing "Yankee Doodle" softly. The other two girls also sing with her. Soon the whole class is watching and at that moment all three girls hold up signs directing the class to the rug for math.

There is nothing extraordinary about this tactic. What is "beyond the subject" about the teacher's technique is that she allowed her students to brainstorm and take charge of an aspect of the classroom learning community that fosters their communication skills and gives them an opportunity to solve a problem collaboratively and quickly. This is as important as learning the skill of measuring angles that was to follow. Ann Bogart (2001) refers to this as "creating spaces where things happen." It is not enough for us to say we are helping our students to be creative problem solvers. We need to provide the space for them to act as problem solvers with personally contextualized problems to ponder.

IN THE HALLWAYS

As a teacher I often found walking my class to and from another location in the school to be particularly challenging. It seemed to me that once students were out of our classroom community boundaries it became easier for them to be rambunctious. I began to use a strategy I heard about at a conference I had attended, and discovered it worked magic—probably for the same reasons discussed above. In the morning, when students arrived at the classroom door, I greeted them with a basket of folded note cards. Students were instructed to take one and write directions on the back side of the card to the school destination listed. For example if the note card read *Art Room*, the student would write out specific, step-by-step directions to reach the Art Room from our classroom door. Students picked a card with a school location on it from a basket in which there were several duplicates for each location. Students wrote or drew their directions to the location on the back of the index cards and handed them in to me without names. I sorted the cards by destination. When we had to go, as a class, to one of the locations, I would choose a reader who would lead the class by reading, one step at a time, the directions written on the given card. For the return trip, a new reader was chosen and the task was to read the directions on the card from the end to the beginning and interpret from this "backward design" how to return the class to our room. The students loved this activity, and as a result of several weeks of participating in following directions that were sometimes confusing and occasionally incorrect, students became more proficient at communicating directions whether written, visual, or verbal.

WAITING GAMES

Another activity for transitioning students in the hallway to another location is to have a set of observation journals by the door. As students leave the room, they take a journal and proceed, in silence, to jot down either shapes, patterns, or anything else they decide to tally on their walk, such as the number of students they pass wearing red shirts or the number of open doors they pass. The observation recordings can be the basis for a class discussion at another transition time, such as teaching intervals I refer to as "the waiting game." "Waiting games" are unplanned, unscheduled times throughout the week when you are caught with a class of students and for whatever reason, you are left waiting: for the buses to be called at the end of the day, for the room mother to arrive with the party cupcakes, to be called to an assembly, or just left with 15 or 20 minutes that do not give you enough time to start a new lesson.

One way I have integrated math thinking with other classroom routines is to incorporate a math problem with daily yoga exercises. Yoga is a relaxing transition that can alter the mood of the classroom. Combining math with yoga stretching creates an excellent math-focused transition. You can pose some yoga-based math problems such as "In the next 86 seconds choose any combination of yoga poses and remember how many seconds you hold each pose" or "In the next 125 seconds perform any combination of yoga poses and record the number of seconds each pose is held. Choose at least three poses and no more than seven." This activity can be altered depending on the grade level you teach and your familiarity with yoga. At the conclusion of the yoga transition problems, take a few minutes to hear some of the choices students made and mark them on a chart kept somewhere in the classroom. The same problem could be posed every day for one week in order to create a long list of combinations. This activity provides math learning in pattern recognition, factors, and time.

As mentioned in the discussion concerning math journals, math dialogue is essential to achieve a deep mathematical understanding. Using a transition that gets the students to talk about math is a way to deepen this understanding. There is one simple activity that accomplishes this. The teacher thinks of a number and the students try to figure out the number using only yes or no questions. Questions such as the following can be used: "Is it a prime number? Is it even/odd? Is it in the hundreds?" This is a quick transition that accomplishes the task of having students think critically about a given number. It encourages them to see numbers as unique things possessing multiple traits.

TRANSITIONING FROM HOME TO SCHOOL

Transitioning from arrival and morning activities to the first learning block of the day is a perfect opportunity to play "Cup." This became a daily morning happening in my room. The initial game began with all the students and me standing in a large circle. We counted off so each person knew their place number. I proceeded to explain we were going to play a game called Cup, which meant we were going to count in a new way. I demonstrated by saying we couldn't say the number 6 because in our new counting system, 6 didn't exist. We were going to count 1, 2, 3, 4, 5, Cup, 1, 2, 3, 4, 5, Cup, etc. We practiced counting around the circle. I then asked the students, "If we count around the circle, starting with the number 1 position, which is mine, with this new counting system every time someone says 'Cup' they must sit down. We will continue counting until there is only one person left standing. Do you have any thoughts about which number position might be left standing?"

Students offer several guesses and we note those. The counting begins. When one person is left standing we record which number position it was.

I then ask, "If we repeat this counting and again start with the number 1 position, what number place will be left standing?"

I know such a question may sound silly, but I have had students respond with answers such as, "It makes a difference how fast or slow we count." If a response such as this is given, we go through the activity as before, only this time count very slowly. When the same person is left standing, students can come to their own conclusions about whether or not speed makes a difference in the outcome. I then query the class, "Which number position do you believe will be left standing if we begin with number position 4 and still count 1, 2, 3, 4, 5, Cup?" Students offer several speculations and then we count until one person is left standing. We record the results on a chart that looks like this:

Beginning Number Position	Number Position Left Standing
16	19

I then ask students, "If we want position number 22 to be left standing, what number position must we start with when we count?"

We continue playing Cup each day and record the results on our chart. Students become proficient at using pattern to theorize an outcome until one day Jenny is absent. Until now the game had been played with 27 students, plus the teacher, making our total 28 positions. I ask the students, "What do you think will happen to our pattern today with only 27 people?" Students offer their thoughts and we begin to count around the circle, beginning with the number 1 position. When the 16th position is not the one left standing, the students ponder the pattern changes. We start a new chart and add a label to the first chart that reads "28 People." We title our newly made chart "27 People." Since this has become a daily morning event, I have placed masking tape number positions on the classroom floor and students stand on a number, beginning with 1. That way if someone is missing, it is easy to determine the positions without beginning the game of Cup by initially counting off to determine the counting positions each day.

Before long, students want to know if the pattern changes in the same way if we add a person, making a new recording sheet labeled "29 People." For this exploration, students invited the custodian in for our morning Cup game.

We continue to play this game each morning, and I await questions to arise from the students' curiosities. Without fail, the following questions emerge:

"Will the pattern stay the same if we double the number of people?" For this exploration we invited the class next door to join us.

"Do even numbers have similar patterns?"

"What happens if we count in Cup and 5 is the number that does not exist?"

This then requires additional labels on our charts, to include the counting base. I go back and add base 6 to the charts already hanging and we create a new chart labeled "Base 5, 28 People" and repeat the game. I play only one or two games of Cup each day and continue until students are no longer intrigued. One year the class continued the game all year and students became quite sophisticated in their pattern predictions. In the process students also learned the beauty of numbers and the predictability of pattern. Mathematics is the science of pattern and order (NRC, 1989) and students learned a practical application of that. Not all transitions are due to school schedules. Occasionally, the need for unexpected transitions may arise that also provide meaningful, innovative, on-the-spot mathematics learning opportunities.

I was sharing the notion of student-led learning with a good friend of mine. Jae teaches third grade and is one of the finest educators I know. She views teaching as a flexible endeavor and began telling me about a recent classroom episode that after several years of teaching was an "aha" for her. Throughout her career Jae's teaching reflections have consistently been connected with understanding the value of letting student interest drive the learning and what that actually looks like in a classroom. As we sat over a Saturday lunch together, she laughed as she related her story.

> I had elaborately prepared an interactive lesson on taxation without representation for my students. It was part of the required curriculum, but I wanted to find a way for the students to understand the concept as it relates to their own lives. I created groups and asked the students to come up with real-life examples of when they felt decisions had been made without their input yet the consequences of the decisions had had a profound effect on them. It was 10 o'clock in the morning and it began to snow. I marched on with my lesson, after a brief acknowledgment of the snow that was falling outside our window. Students were squirming in their seats and whispering among themselves and pointing toward the window. I tried to regain their attention until I realized the futility of learning about taxation in the midst of the first snowfall of the season. It was then that I decided to go with the flow and I asked the class to stop for a moment and said to them, "Everyone put away your work and get your coats on."
>
> I proceeded to lead the class outside with only one instruction: "Take 20 minutes to play and explore in the snow. When I hold up my arms, please return to this spot."
>
> Students romped about, making footprint paths, some trying to catch snowflakes on their tongues, and a few were attempting to make snowballs. Twenty minutes later when I held up my hands, students ran to where I was and excitedly began expressing joy in their snow adventures. They returned to the classroom with a newfound energy to participate in the interrupted taxation lesson.
>
> Later in the day, Jae instructed the students to write math problems about their morning in the snow.
>
> "I made a snow path with my footprints. I had 10 footprint paces. How long was the footprint path?"
>
> "If I could catch 13 snowflakes on my tongue in 1 minute, how many could I catch in 5 minutes?"
>
> "We made a lot of small snowballs. How many snowballs would it take to fill the wastebasket?"

Unexpected but imperative transitions such as the romp in the snow provide teachers with circumstances of connection. By countering student inattention with a response that respects student interest the teacher is conveying a significant message. I am not implying that every time students don't attend to the lesson at hand the teacher should bend to their desired diversions. Yet, the occasion of a first snowfall of the season may warrant such acknowledgment.

TRANSITIONING TO HOME

The end of the day was a particularly chaotic time in the classroom for me with children asking questions, gathering materials, making plans for the afternoon with friends, and some dismissing early. It became difficult to wrap up lessons at this time or to begin anything new. Carol and I tried to utilize these 15 minutes at the end of the day with meaningful math learning. One of the favorite math interludes was a game called "Too High, Too Low." I would secretly write a number on a piece of paper and keep it folded and placed on the blackboard tray.

The numbers 1–10,000 were boldly written at the top of the board. Students took turns around the room trying to guess my secret number. As they offered their guesses, I would write the number in either the Too High side or the Too Low side of the board.

Today's number is 696. Anika says 5,500 for her turn. I write 5,500 under the Too High side. It is James's turn. He calls out 3,000. I write his number under 5,500. It is now Elliot's turn to guess the number. He says 1,000. Again, I write his guess under 3,000 on the Too High side. Sarah suggests 500 and I move to the Too Low side and write her suggestion of 500. Next it is Sam's opportunity to speculate and he calls out 800. I put his number on the Too High side. The board now looks like this:

1–10,000

TOO HIGH	TOO LOW
5,500	500
1,000	
3,000	
800	

Guesses continue to be placed on the appropriate sides of the board until students get closer and closer to narrowing down the secret number. If a student makes a guess that seems to indicate a lack of number sense, I say nothing and put the guess on the board. I have found that over time Too High, Too Low helps students gain a better grasp of number sense. Students are thinking for themselves and learning through discovery without being directly instructed in a game strategy that will help them make efficient and appropriate guesses.

By allowing students to construct their own sense making, in their own time, I believe they feel less stress and develop more confidence in their own abilities.

The challenge of Too High, Too Low is for the class to guess the number with a single round of guesses around the room. As the year progresses the students try to determine the secret number in 15 guesses and then they try to beat that by getting the number in 10 guesses. After several times of playing the game I then have the student who uncovered the hidden number be the person to choose the secret number the following day. It is a much more difficult task to write the guessed numbers correctly in the proper column on the board. I have used this game in every grade level from kindergarten to seventh grade, making the initial range suitable for the grade.

Not all teaching requires talk. The following vignette exemplifies student engagement and learning that occured without words.

"We are going to play a game today but I am not going to tell you the rules of the game. You will have to figure them out for yourself." The teacher places the grid on the overhead and divides the room into two teams: a red team and a blue team.

"Each person will, in order, around the tables, call out two numbers between 0 and 18. This is a silent game. You are not to communicate with one another, but you will be working individually to help your team." Students take turns, the red team followed by the blue team, calling out pairs of numbers. As the numbers are given the teacher makes an X in the team color on the grid. This continues until after several minutes and many Xs being placed on the grid, a series of three Xs in a row is circled by the teacher. A change sweeps over the classroom as students take on a reenergized interest in the game. Now they begin to see the purpose: create three Xs in a row without being sabotaged by the opposing team.

The students watch intently as numbers are called and Xs are placed on the grid. Quietly, they are counting the number of circles produced by their team. Then, totally unexpectedly, the teacher circles another set of three numbers when a fourth is added onto one of the circled three (Figure 4.1).

A new rule has been discovered. You can get another circle appended to your team score merely by inserting an X to either end of an existing circled sequence of Xs. Again, a reinvigorated motivation for playing the game occurs. Students begin to call out pairs of numbers, but now with a defensive tactic as well as an offensive strategy. Student reasoning is raised to another level as thinking becomes more nuanced. Students now strategize which set of numbers will obtain the greatest scoring outcome for their team.

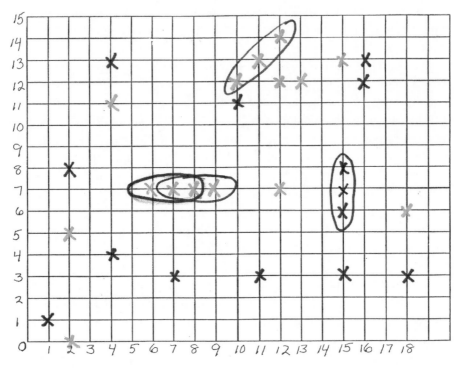

Figure 4.1

USING TRANSITIONS TO REINFORCE CONTENT

Fraction understanding is something that needs continuous scaffolding throughout the year and across the grade levels. Early fractional concepts of ½ and ¼ can begin to take shape in first grade. "I need ½ of the class to line up for lunch." Let the students solve how to accomplish this. The first time you ask them may be chaotic, but over time they will begin to develop important fractional understandings. If you do this often, the whole changes. Five students are absent, so ½ is not the same as it was when the entire class was in school. "I need ½ of the girls to line up today." Again, the whole is not always the same. This helps students to grasp "big ideas" in mathematics. "Fractional parts are equal shares or equal-sized portions of a whole or unit. A unit can be an object or a collection of things. More abstractly, the unit is counted as 1" (Van De Walle, 2007, p. 293). With older grades you could change the fractional requests to a more appropriate problem-solving task: "I need ⅔ of the class to line up." The next day, "I need ⅗ of the class to line up." This could be followed up with a discussion on which is more: ⅔ or ⅗.

Transitions are the hidden moments in the teaching day where we can infuse mathematics reasoning while providing children with enjoyable learning intervals that require thinking. My experience has shown that these "games" become requested activities by the students, which leads me to believe that students also want transition times to be more than lining up and being quiet.

TEACHER AS RESEARCHER THOUGHTS

1. How would you characterize your transitions into math lessons depending on the time of day you teach mathematics? Is the transitioning action more of a focusing activity or an energizing pursuit? How does student engagement differ when math is introduced with a focusing activity instead of an energizing introduction and vice versa?

2. What role does gender play in transition activities? Do some transitions captivate boys more than girls?

3. Think about your own vulnerability as a teacher and the ways in which transitions make you feel more or less vulnerable.

4. Is there a way to design a teacher research agenda that examines the way students' problem solving is affected?

Chapter 5

What Is Real about Homework?

Students almost ran down the hall as the school day began—eager to tell Mr. Spinale the way their parents had solved the homework problem. These second-grade students were given the problem of asking someone at home how they would go about getting an answer to 365 plus 217. They were — *hmm idea* instructed to tell their parents that there is not a "right" way to solve this, but to ask for different ways of thinking about how to solve the problem.

Mr. Spinale gathered the students around the blackboard in the front of the room and wrote the problem on the board.

$$365 + 217$$

Andrew couldn't wait and blurted out, "My mother showed me a new way! She said 300 and 200 is 500. Then she said 60 and 10 is 70—so now she has 570. Now it gets hard. She said 7 and 3 is 10 to make 580 and then she added the last two left over to make 82."

Sasha shared how her sister insisted that she had to line the numbers up on top of each other as she walked to the board to show the class. She wrote the problem like this:

$$\begin{array}{r} 365 \\ \underline{217} \end{array}$$

"My sister said you have to add the 7 and 5 first and you get 12. She told me not to put the whole 12 down, just the 2 and to bring the 1 up on top of the 6. Then I have to add the 6, 1, and the 1 I put on top. This is, ummm-mmm, wait a minute."

John shouts out, "Eight."

Sasha writes the 8 under the 1 and then continues. "Now I add the 3 and 2 and get 5. My answer is 582—the same as Andrew's mother."

Mr. Spinale and his excited students continued to discuss different strategies the children learned from home. After much sharing and discussion about which way students found easiest, Mr. Spinale gave them a new problem to work on with a partner.

"Try this problem with your partner and use any of the ways you learned this morning or come up with a new way."

He wrote 763 + 557 on the board.

This homework task may appear like rote math learning of algorithms at first glance. However, what separates this task from typical homework assignments that merely ask students to complete isolated math problems is two-fold. First, the students did not know how to add three-digit addition problems; therefore, this problem required them to think about possible ways to figure out a solution. Second, and very important, the children were asked to include family members. They were instructed to learn how someone in the family might think about solving this. When I give this assignment in the fourth grade and have students bring in methods for solving a multiplication problem the family strategies vary widely depending on the culture and age of parents or grandparents. It is a means for students to understand that although there is one preferred method for adding or multiplying in school, there are many other possible approaches that have worked for centuries in other cultures.

DEFINING HOMEWORK

Questions regarding homework—how much, what kind, and whether it is used as review or a means to drill students in facts and formulas—are asked by teachers, administrators, and parents alike. The answers to these questions lie in our beliefs and understandings of the purpose of homework. Webster's defines homework as work that is done in one's home. When you look at the root divisions of the word "homework" (home and work), we begin to get a clearer image of what homework might entail. Home is defined as "the place where a person (or family) lives; a place where one likes to be." It is also defined as "of the family household." Work has multiple definitions:

"effort put forth in doing or making something"

"to do, act; an action"

"purposeful activity"

"to exert an influence as, let it *work* in their minds"

"to make a passage as, to *work* through something"

"to mold; shape; form as, she *works* silver"

"to provoke or arouse as, she *worked* herself into a rage"

If we combine these definitions of home and work we can create a depiction of homework that is broader than the current view many hold of homework.

Homework: a purposeful activity that involves action and doing; an action that will engage children and other family members; doing that arouses interest, provokes new thinking, and shapes ideas.

Embracing this representation of homework elicits new challenges for teachers. The task of creating homework assignments becomes greater than finding practice skill review sheets for children to complete at home under the supervision of often overburdened and weary parents. Rethinking homework requires first reflecting on what are the purposes of giving work to be done at home. The purpose of homework can be multidimensional. It involves some review and practice but also should include tasks that necessitate critical thinking and family involvement. If I am sending students home with work to be done in the after hours of school I want that work to be

- building home relationships,
- creating a sense of wonder and curiosity,
- providing opportunities for students to think in new ways,
- developing students' ownership of learning,
- motivating students to want to know more, and
- affording students the space in their lives to organize their own learning goals and responsibilities.

In the pages that follow I will offer examples of homework assignments that address these homework purpose statements.

BUILDING HOME RELATIONSHIPS

Much of the work I have done with parents has involved many discussions that revolve around school policies, teachers, and expectations for children. Inevitably, the conversations always turn to homework. Parents bemoan their perceived role in the homework dilemma. Parents report that after a long day at work they feel put upon to have to teach skills that they often feel incompetent in teaching. Many parents also express frustration in being put in the role of homework police because it creates family discord and arguments. "I have a few hours each day to be with my family and spending that time fighting with my child about finishing homework is not right." Math homework is the one subject that evokes the greatest level of conflict in the home. "My teacher doesn't let me do it that way," "I don't get it," and "She didn't tell us how to do it" are common exclamations heard in many households during the after-dinner-before-bed hours. Internally, parents are dealing with frustrations and feelings of incompetence. Mathematics is typically the subject most people experienced difficulty with themselves in school, and they are terrified of not knowing how to help or apprehensive they might provide the wrong instruction for their children. Such fractious feelings are not conducive to household harmony.

There is no research that claims homework actually leads to higher student achievement in elementary school grades. The truth about homework is that assigning hours of homework does not translate into greater academic success for young learners and might actually be harmful to young minds and increase family stress (Bennett & Kalish, 2006; Kohn, 2006; Kravolec & Buell, 2000). Therefore, we need to think about homework that brings about family harmony and helps students to learn beyond merely practicing skills repetitively.

CREATING A SENSE OF WONDER AND CURIOSITY

"How much water does your family use in one week?" is a homework assignment that requires more mathematics and problem solving than most math worksheet pages I have encountered in my many years of teaching. The problem also calls for individual thinking and family discussion in order to fully investigate this problem. The dialogue that occurs is quite different from one that occurs when parent and child are trying to complete a page of problems that requires a formula or method of solving with a single right answer. The family discussion around how much water they use becomes exactly that: a discussion. There is no "correct" answer or way to solve this question. Each family will have various ways of approaching the question and unique ways to think about how to document their family's water usage. With open-ended tasks such as these is also the probability a student will not be satisfied with a simple answer to the question asked but instead will uncover new problems along the way. "If our family uses X amount of water in a week how much do we use in a year?" "Do other families use more or less water than we do?" "Do we use less water in the winter than in the summer?" "How can my family reduce our water usage?" are only a few of the questions a student may wonder about after investing in solving the original question.

One goal of homework assignments should be to give students a way to connect the mathematics they are learning to real-life dilemmas. If the homework seems "real," students are more willing to take ownership of what they are learning. Creating homework tasks that allow children the unique experience of seeing the value in their own thinking is not as difficult as you might imagine. The problem is often uncomplicated, straightforward, and stated with a single question such as "How much water does your family use?" or "Which cell phone plan is the best buy?" Each of these examples provides students an opportunity to have their thinking critiqued in respectful ways by their peers because the answers necessitate class discussion and explanations of how and why an answer makes sense.

FINDING A BALANCE

It is time for teachers to let go of the notion that students always need to practice mathematics with repetitive problems in order to be mathematically competent and trust that open-ended homework assignments may also fetch equally desirable learning outcomes. There is space in the school year for both. It makes sense to send home practice pages of problems a few weeks prior to taking a high-stakes test. Students need to be exposed to testlike problems in order to become familiar with the format they will encounter during test taking. It also makes good sense to review the procedural and algorithmic strategies that more than likely will be covered on a test. But it is my belief that during much of the year homework assignments can be utilized as opportunities for students to deepen their thinking, to think in novel ways, to become confident in their own problem-solving prowess, and to learn to enjoy learning and discovering mathematics. If you want students to "practice" the formula for volume, give them the problem of figuring out how many grapefruit would fill up their bedroom. In order to solve this problem, volume has to be thought about, but students will discover the properties of volume in figuring out how many grapefruit it will take to fill the room. Some students will approach the problem by thinking about how to cover the floor first and then think about adding layers of surface area. Other students find out how many grapefruit it will take if they stack them one on top of the other to the ceiling and then count row after row of the stacks until they have filled the room. Still other students solve a smaller version by figuring out how many grapefruit will fit into a box and then learn how many boxes it will take to fill the room. In all instances students are learning about volume and how it involves area and height.

HOMEWORK DOESN'T HAVE TO BE DRUDGERY

Miss Andrews is sitting in her rocking chair listening to the explanations her fourth-grade students are sharing about the strategies used to solve last night's homework problem. The problem she gave them to solve was to make a deck of ten cards, numbered 1 to 10, and order them in such a way that you can do the following:

Place the cards face down in a pile. Take the first card and turn it over: it is a 1. Discard the 1 and place the next card, which was the second card, on the bottom of the deck. Turn over the next card on the top of the pile, which is the third card and it should be a 2. Discard the 2 and take the fourth card from the top of the deck and place it on the bottom of the deck. Now take the top card, the fifth card, and turn it over. It should be a 3. Discard the 3 and take the sixth card from the top of the pile and put it on the bottom of the deck. Turn the top card and this time it should be a 4. Discard the 4 and place the next, the eighth card, at the bottom of the deck. Continue doing this and each time a card is turned over from the top of the deck it should follow in order until there is only one card remaining, which should be a 10.

The following discussion illustrates the various strategies used by the students.

Belen: I make blank cards and each time I turned one over I wrote the number it should be on the card in one corner and in the other I wrote the number it was in order.

Melissa: I don't get what you did. How did you know what order it was?

Belen: I kept track on paper like this.

| 1 | discard |

| | put on bottom |

| 2 | discard |

| | put on bottom |

| 3 | discard |

| | put on bottom |

| 4 | discard |

| | put on bottom |

| 5 | discard |

| | put on bottom |

Second round

[6]	discard
[ ]	bottom
[7]	discard
[ ]	bottom
[8]	discard

Third round

[ ]	bottom
[9]	discard

Last card

[10]

Freddy: "I kept trying and if it didn't work I tried it another way. I did this for a long time but I finally got the right order."

David: "I couldn't get it. I tried and gave up. My mother wants to know how everyone else figured it out."

Candace: "I made a chart like this,

[ ] [ ] [ ] [ ] [ ] [ ] [ ] [ ] [ ]

then I skip counted by two's and wrote the numbers in the blanks. The first card is a 1, skip a card, 2, skip a card, 3, skip a card, 4, skip a card, 5, etc.

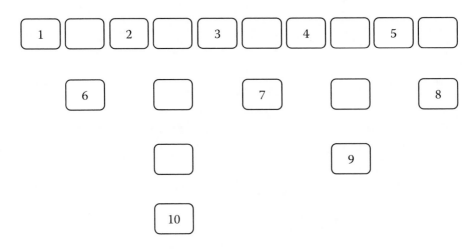

Candace (continued): The final order is then 1, 6, 2, 10, 3, 7, 4, 9, 5, 8.
Aaron: Miss Andrews, can we do more problems like this? It was fun.
Melissa: Yeah. Please.

Students all joined in, asking their teacher to assign more homework problems similar to the one students had just finished discussing. This is a teacher's dream. Imagine having your students beg for more homework?

DEVELOPING STUDENTS' OWNERSHIP OF LEARNING AND MOTIVATING STUDENTS TO WANT TO KNOW MORE

The following homework assignment was given to students in a mathematics methods course that I taught. Each student asked three people to respond to the request below. They were asked to e-mail the results to me using an online asynchronist discussion format.

Circle one of the numbers on the page.

   1   2   3   4

The responses the students reported as well as their thoughts about the results as they posted them online are quite amazing. The entire discussion is displayed below.

The results are in. Twenty-three of you have responded so far and here are the counts:

   6 people chose #1
   28 people chose #2

49 people chose #3
27 people chose #4

What I want you to think about and post your thoughts on is the following: What do you think is going on? What new study would you like to conduct to get more data about this curious study? What do you speculate will be the results from the remaining students in our class who have not yet sent in their results? Why?

Talk to each other online and feel free to conduct another related study. We'll discuss this in class next week. Have fun!

Judy

Forum: 1 2 3 4 results
Date: 11-16-2005 10:11
Student 1

I wonder why most people pick 3. Is it because it's in the middle and a more secure choice? I would be interested to conduct a study with one more choice, the number 5. Would the results be the same? Would most people pick 3 again or would 4 have more? I would speculate that the remaining students would have similar responses, that 3 would be a popular choice. It seems that picking 3 is the trend.

Date: 11-16-2005 10:41
Student 2

When I conducted my survey, one person mentioned that the letter "C" is the most picked answer on multiple-choice tests. That letter happens to be in the same spot that the number "3" is in. I wonder if there is a correlation. I also wonder would people still pick the number "3" if they didn't see the sheet? If you told them to pick a number 1 to 4 over the phone or without the sheet, I wonder if the answers would be the same. I did a few of mine over instant message, and 4/5 of my people said "3." I set it up exactly like the sheet said in the exact same order.

Date: 11-16-2005 13:39
Student 3

I wonder if we replaced the numbers we used with any other numbers (say 5, 6, 7, 8) if 7 would be chosen most frequently? I think it has something to do with the position, rather than just the number.

When I was teaching middle school science, the teachers in our department were asked to devise a grading scale to show how students were performing. The first draft of the scale worked from 1 (performing poorly) on up to 5 (performing excellently). There was a long debate about it once we had thought it through. We talked about the natural inclination to never pick either end of the scale … as teachers we didn't want to give any kid a 1 or a 5 … so we would more than likely end up picking 2, 3, or 4.

Date: 11-17-2005 00:12
Student 4

There seem to be several possibilities why 3 was selected 50% of the time by those asked. To me, the first thought I had was that 3 is the first number that creates ambiguity.

The second thought I had was that a majority of people are right handed. And if they are given this sheet of paper they are going to put it in front of them. To look at all the numbers they are going to have to draw their hand all the way to the right, just past the four. If you hold your pen/pencil in your hand as such, the tip of the pen/pencil is pointing at the 3.

Anyhow. To make this more random, it would make more sense to lay the numbers across the page without a preexisting pattern. Rather, randomly lay them across the page with no consideration for vertical or horizontal spacing. That way the person choosing isn't selecting from a perspective that calls on them to evaluate numbers in a sequentially increasing order.

Date: 11-18-2005 14:50
Student 5

When Judy told us that 3 is overwhelmingly chosen I was very curious as to why and if that would be the case in my study. I actually only had 1 person choose 3. As opposed to some of the other posts in which children were used as test subjects, I chose only adults. Two of the adults were actually a brother and a sister who both circled 2. When asked why they chose 2 they each had the same reason, because it was the sister's birth date! I do agree with Walter that arranging the numbers differently on the page is very interesting and one that would be great to try as is just verbally asking people to choose a number. Conducting those experiments would definitely add more validity to the study.

Date: 11-19-2005 08:22
Student 6

Hmm. Interesting. What is it about the number 3 that causes more people to select that number more than any of the others? I wonder if it is related to social needs; the number 3 is a comfortable number, because the number 1 is alone, and the number 4 is too many? I wonder if it is because of the many associations that we have in our culture to the number 3: 3 strikes, 3 outs in baseball for each team, 3 colors in a traffic light, many dances (i.e., waltz) have 3-counts, 3 wishes, 3 blind mice, 3 little pigs, the 3 bears (Goldilocks), 3 branches of government, Jesus' resurrection on the third day, the Holy Trinity, 3 meals a day, 3 musketeers, 3-ring circus. There are more abstract things that relate to the number 3 as well, like "past, present, future," "morning, noon, and night." There's even a saying, "Everything happens in 3's." I would like to find out more by gathering the following data:

From a list of only odd numbers (say, 1, 3, 5, 7), what number will be selected most?

What are the statistics for number of families (with children) with 2 children, 3 children, 4 children? I think that just in our classroom, most were from families of 5, indicating that the higher percentage of students were from families of 3 children?

What number would most people choose if given the choice between 1, 2, and 4?

I would speculate that the results of the remaining students would be consistent with what has already been submitted, because this collection of data is a gathering of results. It is kind of like "the odds are" that their results will be in line with what's already been gathered.

Date: 11-20-2005 15:43
Student 7

I started to think about the results and exams. Clearly, what everyone has been saying is true. Take the scenario: if you are given a 60-question multiple choice test, and an hour to take it, with options A, B, C, D or 1, 2, 3, 4, or even an E or 5 and at the end of the exam with five minutes to go, most people would choice option C or 3, because that is what we almost naturally do, or as most of our professors have told us to do over the years as a good idea.

I wonder now what if, and I know that on a test this would not happen, but just on a paper like the one given in class, there were other numbers assigned. Such as 50, 51, 52, 53, 54, 55. What would happen? What numbers would be chosen then?

Date: 11-21-2005 12:41
Student 8

I was not surprised to see that 3 was the number picked most often. However, the fact that so few people picked the number 1 did surprise me.

Number 1 has so many positive connotations in our society I would have thought more people would have picked this number. I would be interested to hear about who people asked to participate in the survey and in what way they asked the participants to pick the number. I know in my case I asked a few people while I was rushing off somewhere, and the other two people I asked when I had lots of time and was more relaxed. This may be stretching it a bit, but I do wonder if my demeanor affected the number that my participants choose.

I also agree with those people who have commented about the order of the numbers. I too believe that if we had been asked to cut the numbers out and place them randomly on a surface the results could have been different. I also think it would be interesting to see which numbers people would pick if they were read out loud to them in various orders. That would be an interesting experiment to conduct.

Date: 11-21-2005 15:44
Student 8

I would think that it might have something to do with the visual aspect. If they are reading the number from left to right then 3 is one of the last numbers they read. Also since it is sandwiched between the 1 and 4 it is more visually appealing to look at because of its positioning in the middle. Sometimes, we tend to focus on what is in the middle and forget about the peripheral.

This homework assignment captured and fascinated the students. In the eight student responses shared here you can clearly see how the assignment tweaked their curiosity, created a thirst to learn more, fostered dialogue among peers, and elicited new questions. If we could provide homework experiences that generated similar learning excitement I suspect homework wouldn't create the sense of drudgery it currently does for many students.

The 1 2 3 4 study captured student interest in ways untypical of school homework assignments. Unexpectedly, students' engagement with this problem didn't end with the initial investigation. I had suggested students try a new study if they were interested in taking the study further. I was not expecting the response from students that follows.

Date: 11-27-2005 11:35
Group 1

Lany, Amy and I decided to test the theory that the position of the number on the paper had something to do with what number people circled. We decided to change the page so that the numbers read 1, 2, 3, 4 vertically, as such:

1

2

3

4

When I conducted the original test (numbers arranged horizontally across the page), two left-handers picked the number 2 and three right-handers picked the number 3. This time, I again asked two left-handers and three right-handers (different people). The results were the same for the right-handed people, but not for the lefties. Both left-handed people circled the number 1 this time.

I think that the position of the numbers on the page probably does have something to do with the results. A left-handed person holds his pencil in such a way that it is pointed down the page. A right-handed person holds his pencil so that it is pointed up the page. Therefore, I think it is only natural for a lefty to pick a number at the top and for a right-hander to pick a number towards the bottom. However, this does not explain why my right-handed subjects picked the number 3 instead of 4.

Date: 11-27-2005 15:05
Group 2

Pam and I decided to test whether the placement of letters, rather than numbers, affected the choice made by participants. In other words, we changed two factors in the test: the symbols from numbers to letters (A, B, C, D), and the placement of the letters on the paper from 1 2 3 4 to A B C D.

Prior to conducting the experiment, we predicted that C would be the most chosen letter. This was because of the frequency in which C is usually chosen as an answer, specifically on multiple choice tests. Although we aren't sure why this is so, we thought that it would follow through into the experiment we conducted. We thought that the letter would have more of an impact on the choices, rather than its position on the paper.

Our results were as follows: A - 1; B - 3; C - 5; D - 2.

As you can see, our predictions were correct. More people chose the letter C. But was it the position of the letter, or was it the letter itself? We believe that the letter itself plays more of a role, because the placement of the letters was altered from what people are used to seeing. We thought that people are used to seeing the arrangement as A, B, C, D. Now, it would be interesting to see if we completely mixed up the arrangement, for example, C, A, D, B. Would people choose C now? It would be interesting to investigate.

Date: 11-27-2005 21:27
Group 3

My partner and I decided to write the numbers sequence out of order. Instead of writing numbers 1, 2, 3, 4 like this, we wrote 2, 1, 4, 3. It was interesting because two of my participants chose 2 and the other two chose the number 4. These were the same results I had from the previous test. I know what you are thinking, and yes I asked different people. I wish I asked them for their reasoning, however I did not. All I can say is that for some reason, I like even numbers better than odd. Maybe it is the way they divide into equal groups. I am making a guess, but I feel the order of the numbers did not throw them off. They clearly know the numbers 1, 2, 3, 4. I wonder if we used higher numbers, if order would have an effect on the results. I bet it would, that should be our next experiment, using higher numbers.

Date: 11-28-2005 12:49
Group 4

Penny and I decided to use the same numbers (1 to 4) and place them differently than our first time around. We used the same size and font, but placed numbers as follows:

2

4 1

3

on the paper …
I also asked 5 third-grade students in my class …
my results were:

4 chose #4

1 chose #3

Date: 11-28-2005 15:31
Group 5

Kelly and I conducted a study with eight people using the numbers 6, 7, 8, and 9. Our results are as follows:

6 - 1

7 - 4

8 - 2

9 - 1

We found that 8 was not the most frequently selected number although it was in the same place as the 3 had been in the previous study. We also found that 3 and 7 are both in the middle of the number range and that both are odd numbers, which we think is significant. Kelly also thought that people chose the number 7 because it is a lucky number.

Date: 11-29-2005 11:00
Group 6

To test the placement theory as well as the "letter C" theory I handed out the following sheet to 10 people: C D A B.

My results were:

A = 4 people

B = 0 people

C = 3 people

D = 3 people

This was interesting because 7 out of 10 people chose a letter somehow related to the third number, as in the 1, 2, 3, 4 original survey. The A was in the 3 spot and the C is the 3 spot in letter order.

I would like to conduct this study again and put B in the third spot. This would be interesting I think because no one picked B. I want to know if there is some reason for that or if it was due to it being the letter in the fourth slot. If the B were in the third slot would that be the most chosen letter?

As you can tell from reading the student explanations about their new studies, the interest level has remained high and the problem still leaves them wanting to know more. This assignment has captured the attention of the students while fostering their continued involvement and maintaining a personal appeal in trying to make sense of a phenomenon they do not understand. Once the original question is posed, the investigation takes on a life of its own, depending on the curiosity of those involved. I have had students who become so intrigued with this study that they continue long after the class is finished with the exploration. Students e-mail other classes in different parts of the country and even have expanded to ask people in other countries and in other languages. This is an example of a problem that allows for all students to enter and there is space at both ends of the learning spectrum for differentiation.

PROVIDING OPPORTUNITIES FOR STUDENTS TO THINK IN NEW WAYS

 The following are homework task suggestions that focus on the students and their everyday lives. These can be used as long-term projects or as single homework assignments. I have included two lists: one for younger learners in grades 1 through grade 3 and another for students in grades 4 through 6. Either list could be modified to accommodate learners in any grade.

Grades 1 through 3

- Ask 10 people, "What is your favorite cookie?" Tally the choices.
- Sort the forks and spoons in your home. Make a graph that shows what you found.

Before you assign this homework, read *What Comes in 2's, 3,s, and 4's?* by Susan Aker and Bernie Karlin.

- Find things in your home that come in 2's, 3's, 4's.
- Take one paragraph of the newspaper and circle all the
  - a's in red
  - e's in blue
  - i's in green
  - o's in black
  - u's in orange

Tally the results. Do you think you will find the same thing if you do this again with another paragraph?

- Start at your door. Walk 100 steps. Make a map of where you walked.
- How many days until your birthday?
- Count out 100 popped popcorn kernels and 100 M&Ms (or raisins, paper clips, …). Make a list of everything you notice.
- Make a paper airplane from the directions on the paper. Test-fly the plane. What is the longest distance you can make it fly?
- Try to find a way to change the airplane so it will fly a longer distance.
- Make a new airplane design and compare flying distances.
- Compare differences in frozen, canned, and fresh packages of vegetables in your home.
- List 10 things in your home that cost less than $1.00.
- List 10 things that cost more than $10.00.

Grades 4 through 6

- Plan a special dinner that you will cook for 35 hungry relatives. Your budget is $100.00. You need to decide on recipes, make the ingredients list, and prepare a timeline for preparing the dinner.
- How far do you walk in one day?
- What does it cost you to feed and care for a dog for a year?
- Make a floor plan to scale of any room in your home. Now design a new room arrangement for the space.
- Make a graph of your family's favorite foods.
- What day of the week will it be in 37 days? 89, 451, 1000 days?
- Make a Venn diagram of the food in your refrigerator.
- Find a real-life example of the following fraction: ½ of ¼ .
- How much paint would you need to paint your room?
- Plan a 4-day family vacation that costs less than $800.00. Include travel, food, entertainment, and lodging costs.
- How much time does each member of your family spend (reading, watching TV, talking on the telephone, etc.) each day?

A parent told me that her daughter insisted on taking charge of planning the family trip to Grandma's after doing the vacation homework assignment. The parent was delighted that her daughter was feeling ownership of her learning in this way.

GIVE ME THE FACTS

Isn't it important for students to learn their facts? This question is the one most frequently asked by parents and teachers alike. The answer is simple—yes. Knowing addition/subtraction and multiplication facts helps students to solve problems more efficiently than if they didn't know them. Not knowing "the facts" makes problem solving more tedious and often bogs students down in the lower-level calculation part of problem solving rather than spending time thinking about what the problem is asking and how to solve it. However, the problem in many classrooms is that the focus of learning becomes memorizing facts and algorithms. A concentration on facts is one of the reasons why students will see a word problem and immediately start to compute without taking critical thinking time to understand the problem before they begin. If we find interesting and creative ways to have students learn their facts as homework, more classroom time can be allotted developing problem-solving and critical thinking skills. Parents also want to feel as though they are helping with their child's homework and math facts are a familiar part of the curriculum that doesn't intimidate parents. The following are a few suggestions to get you to think about math fact homework in new ways:

- Create a board game that will help you learn your multiplication facts and play it with a family member.
- Make a set of flashcards for your addition facts and practice them at home with another person.
- Make a puppet show where the characters are learning their facts.
- Create a game idea for us to use at recess that will help the class learn their facts.
- Write a multiplication rap to share in class.

AFFORDING STUDENTS THE SPACE IN THEIR LIVES TO ORGANIZE THEIR OWN LEARNING GOALS AND RESPONSIBILITIES

The kind of problems given is one aspect of the homework quandary. How often teachers should assign homework is another piece of this puzzle. I have found that one of the most frequently heard complaints from teachers is related to homework: "How do I get them to hand in homework?" "I'm tired of excuses and soccer practice interference," "I've got to call Dan's parents and let them know he isn't doing his homework." My team teaching partner Carol and I decided to introduce a weekly homework packet as a way to solve these homework issues. We put together a series of homework assignments—something from each content area—and handed them to the students in a folder on Thursday. The packets were due back on Wednesday morning. Wednesday morning was our "homework discussion" time in class. We would gather on the rug and take each assignment and share solutions and ideas. It became a lively few hours as the children were invested in their solutions and often made comments such as, "My dad can't wait to hear how everyone else thought about this."

Another benefit to the homework packets was the disappearance of homework excuses. It became the students' responsibility to organize their week and make a plan to complete the homework on time. If soccer practice fell on a Tuesday they needed to have the homework completed by Monday night. When we gathered for the discussions on Wednesday morning, all the children had a recording sheet to check off whether they had completed the assignment or not. These discussions were lively. Students were encouraged by their peers and teachers to ask questions, to explain their reasoning, and to make their thinking public. Seymour Sarason (2004) avows you cannot make the claim a student is thinking critically if he doesn't ask questions. If homework was not completed the sheet would be added to the next week's folder for the parent to sign. After the first few weeks we had a 100% homework completion rate. Parents spoke with us about how much they liked the homework policy. They also said the first few weeks were difficult as the children learned they needed to plan ahead and could not leave everything until Tuesday night. But the procedure allowed for individual family schedules and their children enjoyed having control over when they had to do homework.

In an attempt to keep the homework playing field level, Carol and I decided to start a "Homework Club." Homework Club is a strategy to assist those students who may not have an adult at home to talk with about the homework assignments. We set aside Monday lunch/recess time for anyone who wanted to "check in" about the week's homework packet and join us for a Homework Club luncheon meeting in the classroom. As we ate our lunches, we would brainstorm ideas about the tasks for the week and provide an idea boost if that was needed. On occasion students would need an adult to participate in a homework assignment, such as "teach someone at home something you have learned in mathematics." We had a committed group of regulars in the club and occasional members who would attend on specific Mondays with very explicit homework needs. We suspect we had some students who joined us because they enjoyed eating lunch in the calm and quiet of our classroom.

TEACHER AS RESEARCHER THOUGHTS

1. Are there different homework problems that appeal to different children?
2. What is the experience of students who participate in Homework Club?
3. Survey teachers, parents, students, and administrators about their views on homework.
4. In what ways does making changes in homework assignments change students' learning motivations?

Chapter 6

How Do I De-Fang the Test?

Jorge yawns. Erika scratches her poison ivy: first her chin, then her wrist, then back to her chin. Andrew's face is contorted, and Jamal pulls his sweatshirt over his head. The room looks stark, sterile, and lifeless. The tables that were clustered yesterday with chattering groups of four or so students are separated today into isolated units. They are two at a table, lined up in rows like city blocks, one behind the other, with cardboard dividers to prevent the students from sharing and working together. Quiet stalks the room. We've spent the year building and creating a sense of community. How ironic. What must the children be thinking? Or are they bewildered and not thinking at all?

Jorge is rocking back and forth and Jamal is putting his forehead onto his test booklet. I sense Jamal's frustration and cannot help. Roger is standing on his chair. He finds it difficult to concentrate for extended periods of time. Charlie raises his hand and I go over to him. He whispers to me, "There is no number 22 in my book." I show him where the number 22 is and he leans forward to continue, staring at Alisha in front of him instead of at his test booklet. Anthony proudly struts over to me to announce he is finished and to ask if he can go to the reading corner. I have to tell him no, that he must remain in his seat until the time is up.

What a contrast to our classroom of the day before.

"Stop. Put your pencils down and close your test booklets."

The class is lining up to go to lunch, and I overhear Jorge as he turns around to face Charlie. "How'd ya do?" he asks.

Charlie grimaces and answers, "They didn't ask me any of the stuff I know."

There is a depth of knowing that comes from stillness, both of mind and of body. The life of a teacher offers rare moments of stillness. I wrote this classroom observation the day my students were taking the National Assessment of Educational Progress (NAEP) test, often referred to as "the nation's report card." It was the first time I had nothing to do except monitor students quietly writing at their seats. My observations that day have changed how I think about assessment to this day. It seems that what we need to consider in assessment of learning is what students know and understand, not what some outsider determines is necessary to know at that prescribed learning juncture. We have lost our navigational bearings regarding tests. The closer to the student and the classroom that the test is situated, the more meaningful the information will be to the learner and teacher. Leave the standardized, norm-referenced test results to enlighten administrators and policy makers, and leave the job of teaching and learning to the front-line participants.

I read this vignette to undergraduate and graduate teacher education students in order for them to think about the student perspective of test taking. I believe that as teachers and administrators we have a huge burden that entails finding the delicate balance between learning and successful test taking. Though maintaining such a balance is not an easy task, I believe we can provide rich learning environments for students and still prepare them for taking standardized tests that have enormous, long-term implications. The trick is to keep the power priority in proper alignment. A one-day testing snapshot does not adequately assess what a student knows or how well a single teacher's efficacy compares to that of other teachers. Teaching and learning are vastly influenced by particular circumstances of context and require evaluation over time and multiple means of assessment.

More often than not the kind of instruction children receive, what is taught, and the amount of time a teacher feels liberated and unrestricted in order to deviate from a predetermined time table of instruction are decided today by the need to be accountable on standardized tests. Such tests are viewed by those who call for more stringent accountability as the only means by which teachers, schools, and students can be held accountable for learning that does or does not occur. This is a narrow lens by which to assess learning, but nevertheless, it is often the reality for many classrooms. Strategies for "de-fanging" the dreaded test require more than implementing a series of test prep strategies. Because the goal of this book is to assist teachers and administrators in their work I examine immediate and long-term implications of testing for learners and also explore alternative forms of assessment that inform all testing stakeholders. High-stakes testing situations remain a powerful and dominant determiner of a student's learning trajectory, and, therefore, suggestions for how to help students prepare for test taking will be woven throughout this chapter.

In order to de-fang testing anxiety, this chapter considers alternate ways of conceptualizing student learning and offers a theory of assessment and accountability that is situated within the learner rather than by forces imposed from outside. Standardized tests are designed to measure learning sound bytes and not the long-lasting learning most teachers hope to achieve in classrooms. Standardized tests are a means to measure student learning with consistency and from one student to another, one school to another, one state to another, and one country to another. Often this translates to an emphasis on memorization instead of understanding because the latter is not easily measurable by any standardized system. When learning, however, is focused on thinking rather than on the passing of tests, students develop broader conceptions of what constitutes learning. Taking the view of cognitive and sociocultural theorists (Vygotsky, 1978; Wood, Bruner, & Ross, 1976), the core principles that knowledge is constructed and that the process is a function of social interactions embedded in the learner's cultural sphere, then it becomes the teacher's responsibility to scaffold learning through formative assessment as the learner develops understanding. The classroom assignments and work take on more value because the tasks are more meaningful. This, in turn, allows for assessment of a greater range of abilities and knowing. Saljo's (1988) study of university students found that a constructivist approach to teaching and assessment led to students making more comparisons, more evaluations, and more sophisticated structures to their answers when being assessed. I believe the same holds true for learners of any age. The learning outcomes depend on the messages being delivered about what matters. "What does this teacher want me to know?" and "How will she judge me?" are the questions even young learners have figured out about the learning game.

If we want a different learning focus in our classrooms it is our responsibility to stop reinforcing the traditional model of what counts. If we continue to have learning be a "point system" (Huhn, 2005), where scores and grades are valued over understanding, we are reinforcing the idea that students are only in school to accumulate points. This is best exemplified with the "extra credit syndrome." A student is often not receiving the extra credit for deeper understanding or knowledge gained, but for doing something further in order to boost a grade.

SELF-EVALUATION: THE CRITICAL
REFLECTIVE LEARNER KNOWS BEST

Self-evaluation is a research-based effective way for individuals and groups to assess their learning by building a relationship to the learning process in unique ways. First, a learner must recognize her critical role in the assessment/evaluation of her learning. Second, the learner *must* reflect on what constitutes learning and evidence of learning. Throughout the school year students engaged in self-assessing assume conscious and explicit ownership and accountability for choices and decisions concerning their learning. One way to take ownership of the process is by asking questions such as, "What is it that I need to know and what must be done in order to advance my thinking in this topic?" "Has the way I think about what I am learning changed, shifted, or strengthened?" "What evidence can I provide that supports my claims of learning?"

As students become stewards of their learning the classroom shifts from an authority-driven, teacher-driven power structure to a community of learning in which the teacher is a participant offering another critical voice or perspective for the community of learners to consider. The teacher's role is one of learning caretaker, the one monitoring how individual learning needs are met, how curriculum requirements are addressed, and how the collective learning of the community is being nurtured.

The goal of self-assessment is for teachers and students to work toward critical conversations. This can help ensure that all learners have opportunities to communicate ideas that are contemplated, tested, and argued so that individual and community thinking can blossom.

We cannot assume that all children have the same set of prior learning experiences or shared learning goals on which they place their learning. Therefore, how can we judge each student with the same set of understandings and expectations or put them on a plane or continuum that sorts their learning into piles of yes/no, gets it/doesn't get it, understands/does not understand? Self-assessment offers a way to hold students accountable for an explanation of what it is they know and understand and how they know that they understand it. Through self-assessment we have a vehicle for fostering habits and values of scholarship as integral features of the school environment.

Students should have access to the learning that occurs when they think about what has been learned. If we believe learning is an active process of making sense of and shaping and developing ideas that are unique to each individual's learning, to allow only the "teacher" to decide what each learner has learned deprives each learner of a valuable step in the learning journey. If we are searching instead for active student involvement, the kind that necessitates relational understandings and connected learning in which personal and collaborative experience are valued more than authoritarian pronouncements, then the learner is in the best position to explain those relational understandings and connections.

This is possible for learners of all ages, even with very young kindergarten children. It begins with the expectation that the learning process is individual and learners are to ask questions, of themselves and others, that will aid them to propel thinking in new directions.

"What is it you are wondering about?"

"What do you think you need to do to find out?"

"What did you learn?"

"What new questions do you have?"

"What helped you to understand?"

"Have you talked to anyone else about this?"

I have witnessed 4- and 5-year-old children engaged in an exploration of balls and ramps. It is incredible to observe a group of 19 young learners as they work to understand slope, speed, angles, friction, height/distance ratios, and equilibrium concepts. No two children found identical questions as they explored and explained their findings and wonderings. Without being told what to learn, these young students learned sophisticated mathematical truths and owned the process. Each child was able to clearly talk about what he or she discovered and what helped to make those discoveries.

MATH PORTFOLIOS

While I was at Lesley College, I was involved in a project to support teachers in their efforts to initiate reform in the teaching of mathematics. I served as a mentor for three Massachusetts teachers who agreed to abandon the use of mathematics textbooks as the sole instructional guide for their mathematics curriculum. Instead, we focused on the following goals of NCTM's *Curriculum and Evaluation Standards for School Mathematics* (1989): to help children become mathematical problem solvers, to encourage them to communicate mathematically, to teach them to value mathematics, and to create an environment in which students may begin to build confidence in their own abilities. Two of the teachers taught fourth grade and one teacher taught fifth grade. Because all three teachers had agreed to give up their traditional math texts and teach for a year using a variety of materials, I committed myself to being in each of their classrooms one day a week and to assist them in designing a comprehensive, yet organic math curriculum that was integrated with other disciplines as well as with student interests. Each teacher met with her respective principal and superintendent in order to obtain permission before agreeing to participate in this project. One principal agreed only on the condition that a well-thought-out assessment plan would accompany the project. This principal's mandate was the motivation for me to seek expertise and collaboration from Dennie Palmer Wolf of Harvard's Performance Assessment Collaboratives for Education (PACE). Together, we developed a process to assist this group of teachers in creating a math portfolio system.

The portfolio model I include here is the result of a year's collaboration among Dennie, the three teachers, and myself. In this assessment model it becomes the student's job to find the evidence of learning. In so doing, what we discovered was a shift in learning ownership that took place over the course of the school year. With a consistent focus on understanding, students had taken on the responsibility of assessing their own learning in relation to the NCTM's standards as a way by which to assess that learning, show where they had attained understanding, and see where they needed to deepen their learning in order to gain greater understanding.

Each student was given a packet of post-its®. Using the NCTM standards they were asked to go through their portfolios and put post-its labeled with each of the 11 math standards. Geometry, for example, was attached to portfolio entries that they believed documented learning of geometric understanding. Once students did this step in the assessment process they made a list of which standards they could provide evidence of understanding and growth and a list of the standards for which they did not have proof of understanding. After studying their lists, they were asked to write a reflective entry explaining how they intended to focus on these areas next year. This is a powerful tool as it delivers the message to students that learning is not something imposed on them. They have a responsibility in the process to attain learning outcomes and not merely figure out what the teacher wants.

The portfolio model consists of the seven entries listed below. Each entry was designed to reflect the scope of mathematics learned and to allow each student choices in order to document individual learning experiences.

Cover Letter—This may either be in the form of a mathematical autobiography or a letter to the teacher reflecting on the mathematical experience they had during the year.

Group Project—The group will decide on a piece of work and write a group summary of their group's effort and work. This will include how the group worked toward a solution, any multiple strategies used, discoveries they made or were unable to make, and any conclusions they arrived at as a group. Together, the group conferences and presents their work to the teacher.

Pattern Piece—This piece must show evidence of using pattern to solve a mathematical problem and include an explanation of how the discovery was arrived at.

Personal Choice Selection—The student may choose any additional piece of work to include in the portfolio and include a reflective essay on why this piece was chosen and how it contributes to the mathematical learning of the student.

Revision Piece—The student may choose any piece of work to revise and include both the original and the revised versions with an explanation of the changes and why the student made the revisions.

Evidence of Mathematical Growth—This entry will include two pieces of work the student believes show evidence of deepened mathematics understanding.

Teaching Sample—The student will teach someone a mathematical concept and the entry will include an explanation of what was taught, the methods used to teach it, and an evaluation of the process. If possible, include a response paper from the person being taught.

From September until April of the school year I made weekly visits to each of the classrooms involved. During May and June these visits increased to twice a week in each room. The classroom visit was followed with time for the teacher and me to reflect on the lesson and to talk about where to take the instruction from that point; to discuss what was happening in the school and with parents; and to see what she determined was successful with the week's mathematics teaching, as well as discuss concerns she had about teaching without the textbook.

As a group we met once a month after school for three hours. During school vacations we met earlier in the day and worked through lunch. I conducted interviews with each of the teachers and kept field logs of each classroom visit. The following are excerpts from the interviews and field logs.

> They're working with the concepts and owning them. They're making the connection as opposed to the textbook where I really don't think they would have. Learn and forget. This is learn and remember. And use and apply. It's the higher-level thinking that I am amazed with. I think I'm learning two major things. Number one, how capable students' minds are—how fertile they are. And how we don't tap into them enough. And secondly, I'm learning humility. I don't have to have the right answer all the time—that we're on a road of discovery together and all I really need to know is the direction in which to guide them and assess whether they are on the road. They are just amazing me with the higher-level thinking. I've taught 16 years of fourth grade and this is my fourth year teaching fifth grade. The thoughts coming from them are because they have been allowed to express them and to wonder. (Mary interview; McVarish, 1994, p. 19)

> What I really love is in the beginning they used to argue. They used to sit and always say their answer was right and wouldn't listen to anyone else. Now they ask and they ask other people, other students how they got that answer. They're open to other students' approaches. (Gail interview; McVarish, 1994, p. 19)

> I became less fearful of being "divorced" from the text. Best of all is the children's reaction to math now—they looked forward to it. (Ellie journal, October 21, 1992)

> I think probably the kids are learning how to cooperate and how to work together to perform a task. I think they are also learning the process of solving problems and the process of multiplication and the process of addition and why $3 + 5 = 8$ or $4 \times 6 = 24$ and they can concretely see the results and the processes that they are using. (Ellie interview; McVarish, 1994, p. 19)

From my field log:

> Mary called. I have this to share with you. Hillary came in to class Tuesday morning. She had made a graph while listening to the debates (Presidential) the night before. She made a tally mark each time one of the candidates got applause. She brought it in to share with the class. Mary was so excited. This is definitely what teaching should be. (McVarish, 1994, p. 18)

The new approach to teaching and learning mathematics became cemented for these three teachers once they were able to recognize and internalize how the learning of their students differed in significant ways from their prior teaching practice. The evidence clearly showed that teachers believed they had engaged in teaching mathematics that helped their students to make sense out of what they were learning rather than memorizing a finite set of math rules and algorithms.

STRATEGIES FOR REVIEWING SKILLS

Morning Problems

Denise, a friend of mine who taught fifth grade, responded to my question of how she dealt with the testing preparation issue with a well-thought-out plan to help students do well on standardized tests. Denise explained that she did not want to give up her inquiry-based teaching style and become a teacher who spends most of the classroom time feeding students strategies and formulas for successful test taking. She decided a few years ago that she would begin the school year with a systematic approach to this problem. She distributed black-and-white composition notebooks to each child and instructed them to put their names on their "morning work" notebooks. Each morning she would write three or four math problems on the board and three or four grammar sentences or phrases.

Students were to choose any two of the math problems and also pick two grammar sentences to correct. She explained to the students that the problems would vary in both content and difficulty. "We have good days when we feel energetic. On those days, we think we can conquer the world. We also have days when we are feeling less able for a variety of reasons; maybe the family pet died, you were at Aunt May's until late and didn't get much sleep, or maybe you just want to tackle a less challenging problem that day. I trust that you will make the right learning choices for you. These morning problems are our way of working to get ready for the test at the end of the year. If we do this each day from now until April, you will each get the review you need and you will have been the one in control of the process."

Denise put the problems on the board the next day and the students eagerly chose their problems for that day. After lunch was Denise's designated time to go over the problems. Students gathered on the rug and she would ask, "Who did the first problem? Would anyone like to share a method for solving it?" Students shared and discussed solution strategies for each of the problems. If no one chose a problem, Denise would say, "We'll put this up on another day."

At the end of each week Denise would ask the students to write a brief paragraph about their morning work choices: why they chose the problems they did and where they feel confidence and where they need more work. Denise's approach to test prep allowed students to take ownership of their learning and to know what they needed to continue to work on. This also allowed students who chose easier problems to listen to the strategies their classmates employed to solve the more difficult problems and perhaps gave them the tools to choose similar problems in the future.

Wallpaper Skill Border

Teachers have said to me that their biggest fear in teaching projects and problem solving is that they will lose focus and not cover the necessary skills students will be tested on in the spring. One suggestion I learned from a veteran teacher who harbored similar fears but who did not want to give up teaching in a way she believed was best for her students. My friend made a list of each distinct skill her students might encounter on the test in both language arts and mathematics, such as two-digit multiplication and writing a friendly letter. She made a wallpaper border from varied colored construction paper with each skill boldly written in black marker on an 8 × 5 strip.

She posted these strips on the top of the walls all around the room. The skill border was a constant reminder for both her and her students as they worked on projects and solved problems. It was not uncommon for one of her students to say, "Hey, we just did double-digit multiplying when we figured out how much it would cost to feed a cat for a year." About once a month my friend would do an informal inventory of the skills she had covered and those she still hadn't touched on. It was a simple system of accountability that she found was a benefit to her and the students.

Three-Week Countdown

As the dreaded test approached, a strategy I used in my fourth-grade classroom was to explain to the students they would be taking a standardized test in three weeks. I talked with them about the purpose of the test, who would be taking it, and how we were going to prepare to take the test.

Because the students would not be allowed to work in groups or talk to one another during the test we rearranged our room to simulate the required test-taking procedures. Desks were put in rows. We took each mathematics topic, such as fractions, double-digit multiplication, and problem solving and spent a few days reviewing computation strategies and procedures related to the concept area. The homework for the three weeks became worksheets with pages of problems that resembled the format students would encounter in taking the test.

MY FOURTH-GRADE EXPERIENCE

I want to share my own personal experience of teaching students to take a standardized test. I team-taught 54 fourth-grade students with another teacher. We were two of the five fourth-grade classrooms in our school. The other three teachers were more traditional in their teaching styles and relied heavily on using textbooks and direct instruction to help students learn. We were necessarily apprehensive regarding the test results for our class. If our students did not perform as well as other fourth graders we would most likely be asked to abandon our "no textbook" style of teaching and to comply with more traditional methods. It was certainly our belief that if you teach children how to solve problems and give them ample opportunity to engage in dialogue around thinking and reasoning, such skills would enable students to do well on a test even if we hadn't spent the entire year drilling them with formulas and facts. Yet, in all honesty, we were petrified. What if our approach didn't prepare students in the ways we had hoped? We would have done them a terrible disservice.

It takes a few months from the time the test is administered until the results are delivered to the schools. Carol and I decided "what would be would be." We had done what we believed was the best for the students, and we would face the results with similar resolve. Early in June we learned the test results were in the principal's office. Hurriedly, we made our way down the hall to check. After what seemed like hours of reviewing our class and comparing the scores of the other three fourth-grade classrooms, we sighed a huge sigh of relief. Our students had outscored all other classes in problem solving by a wide margin and scored better on concept development than the others. We were slightly lower, but not enough to be significant, on the content section of short answer, memorization of facts. Yahoo! We were ecstatic. We reported the news to both our students and their parents. The best part for us was the confidence with which we taught during our second and third years of team teaching with a sense of surety that we did not have in the first year.

HELPING STUDENTS KEEP TESTS IN PERSPECTIVE

It is difficult for teachers and administrators to keep the testing frenzy in balance. It is no easier a challenge for children to maintain a healthy perspective relative to testing. One way to help students do this is to keep communication open about why they must take tests, what the tests mean for their future learning pathways, and what information the tests give us and what we don't learn from such testing practices. I have used children's literature as a means to stimulate discussions about these testing issues.

First Grade Takes a Test by Miriam Cohen provides a perfect venue for talking about what happens when a student does well or poorly on a test and the implications for the rest of the class when a single test taker is identified or labeled in particular ways. This book also raises questions about the test questions and how different people may interpret them.

Hooray for Diffendoofer Day! by Dr. Seuss, with a little help from Jack Prelutsky and Lane Smith, celebrates learning that is unique and "out of the box" and demonstrates how learning in less traditional ways does not hinder test taking and may even allow students to perform well.

Testing Miss Malarkey by Judy Finchler pokes fun at how an entire school community that is obsessed with student performance on standardized tests spends time in preparation for test taking. This book is a light-hearted, sarcastic lens into society's appetite for accountability and testing.

HELPING TEACHERS KEEP
ASSESSMENT IN PERSPECTIVE

The following "authentic voices" both support the philosophy that learning assessments need not be punitive. The first voice is from a student in graduate school reminiscing about a kindergarten assessment and the second is from a principal as she greets her teachers on the first day of school.

Tyson was a graduate student in an educational foundations course that I taught as part of the Fast Track Teacher Education Program at New York University. The following one-act play is Tyson's response to an assignment in which students were asked to recall an assessment experience. Tyson's minimalist interpretation of a memorable learning experience raises important questions for all of us in the field of education.

Dear Miss Hand,

I have written a one-act play for you to think about, titled SLOPPY ASSESSMENT.

SCENE: Kindergarten, circa 1990. C. R. Weeks Elementary School. Miss Hand, a middle-aged woman with blue eye makeup and red lipstick, presides over her classroom. Tyson, a shy 5-year-old, listens intently at his desk.

MISS HAND: Now class, I want you to take a few minutes to work on your drawing projects quietly at your desks while I do work at my big teacher desk.

STUDENTS *(in unison):* Yes, Miss Hand.

Miss Hand hobbles over to her desk and proceeds to shuffle and grade papers, oblivious to her students, who begin working diligently. Tyson begins working hard on his drawing, coloring in the shapes with crayons. He even puts his first and last name on the top of his paper, something he wasn't able to do before elementary school. When he feels he can add nothing more to the piece, he walks triumphantly up to Miss Hand's desk and presents his work of art.

MISS HAND *(examining the paper briefly):* Mm, no. This won't do. It's too sloppy. Go back and fix it.

Miss Hand returns to her grading. Without a word, Tyson walks slowly back to his desk, his lower lip quivering. As he pulls out a fresh piece of paper and starts over, he cries quietly to himself.

CURTAIN.

I hope you take the message to heart.

Sincerely,
Tyson Schrader

This may evoke protestations from many and not at all be a depiction of our classrooms. Tyson has, however, left us with questions to ponder: What is the role of scaffolding for students in order to help them improve? What sorts of judgment do we place on the work of others without consideration for where — but with consider they might be in the learning process? Is it more effective to concentrate on what one can do to help them get better than on what they can't do, which often stifles progress?

Here is a letter from Rosemary Mills Vickery, a dear friend who had embarked on her first year as principal of a middle school. As she reflected on the address she gave to her new teaching staff her aspiration was to offer words of support in a message that clearly depicted her teaching and learning philosophy.

> As the school year begins, it seems an appropriate time to start the conversation once again about what's important to us as a school community. Schools are no longer free to construct an individualized curriculum suitable to their student population, but are now tied to teaching standards that meet the criteria set by our state and No Child Left Behind legislation. This is not necessarily a bad thing, but it is all the more reason why we need to discuss what we believe and value about learning in our own school.
>
> First and foremost we are a "learning" community. That means we are a group of people interested in, dedicated to, and focused on learning as it applies to our students as well as to ourselves. I emphasize that because I want us to get away from the notion of "we covered it." Too often I hear teachers make statements similar to this one: "I covered that in my class, but half the kids didn't get it." Sadly, it is often the case that the teacher didn't stop to find out why the students "didn't get it," but felt pressured to move on in order to meet the curriculum guidelines before the school year ended. I don't want us to be that kind of a school.
>
> It's our responsibility to design classroom situations where active learning takes place and students feel confident to take risks. When schools were training students for work in factory assembly lines, rote memorization and routine task work were the norms for classrooms. We no longer live in that world. Today's students will be asked to think critically about global problems and develop creative solutions with limited resources. We need to develop their skills so that they can do that. We need to create a program where students are routinely asked to think and figure things out for themselves (with your guidance, of course), so that they can develop that deeper conceptual understanding.
>
> Nowhere is the need to develop critical thinking skills more evident than in mathematics classrooms. As a fifth-grade math teacher I can remember a time when a student told me, "Mrs. Vickery, this is really hard, my brain hurts." I replied something along the lines of "That's great, because when your brain is puzzling over how to do something, that's when you're really learning." Our math classes have to become places where students apply the skills they've been taught by you to real-life problems. We need to encourage our students to use their knowledge to make sense out of problem situations and work toward accurate and efficient solutions, and that doesn't mean they do that in lock step, or all the same way. We need to teach kids that there are many ways to correctly solve problems and all have validity. It's application, not memorization, that leads to this. Recent research supports this; we know that if kids are actively involved in learning and thinking, they retain the skills. They become the kinds of learners that may not know the answer right away, but are willing to explore ways to find it, and they use the tools and skills learned in class to achieve success.
>
> I would be remiss if I told you that our scores on the state tests shouldn't matter. They do. In my role as principal of this school I have to pay attention to the big picture and those scores are definitely a part of that. But I firmly

believe that if we create classrooms where kids are actively engaged in learning, where they question how and why things happen, where the emphasis is on developing meaning and understanding, then the performance on state tests and other assessments will take care of itself. We shouldn't be teaching to the test, we should be teaching the learners in front of us every day. I could go on and on about this, I guess if I had to put it all in a nutshell, it would be similar to Bill Clinton's campaign slogan, when he ran against George Bush, Sr.: "It's the economy ..." For us as a school, I'd like our campaign slogan to become "It's all about thinking and learning!"

Let's have a great year!

Rosemary explicitly gave an image of how a school community is more than a collection of classrooms. Sharing a commitment to an ideal is the same as everyone pushing the cart in the same direction. When teachers work together to infuse mathematics reasoning into their curriculum students receive a harmonious message regarding the kind of mathematics learning that is valued and that learning to be a critical thinker entails questioning and hard work. Passing a test becomes a by-product and not the goal.

IN ADDITION **TESTING STORY**

The *In Addition* afterschool program provides us with two vignettes on testing. The first vignette is about how we helped parents and students reduce anxiety as testing day approached. An evening was designated for parents and students to come together with the *In Addition* staff in the school library for a test-prep dinner meeting. Pizza was provided as well as sample test booklets for students. The evening began with a review of simple test-taking techniques. Parents were asked to watch and not to coach as the students took the 20-minute practice test. Parents were asked to observe how their children approached problems and to jot down their thoughts and suggestions on a piece of paper to be shared with their child after the practice test was completed.

The discussion between parents and children that followed was informative. Students talked about how they felt while taking the test, which types of problems caused them frustration, which problems they found easy, and parents shared their insights: "I noticed you spent a long time on a few problems. Could you have left them blank and come back to them in the end if you had time?" and "I liked how you went back and checked all the answers when you finished. You found a mistake. How did that make you feel?" The dialogue was rich and lively. Parents expressed their gratitude at the close of the meeting. Most of the parents attended because they want to help their children do well and often feel helpless or unsure of how to help. We reviewed for the parents some ways for them to provide support for their children during the week of testing:

- Make sure your child gets to bed early.

- Breakfast is important. Provide a healthy morning meal on test days.

- Review with your child but do not make the review stressful. The test is stressful enough without added pressure from home.

- Build your child's confidence. Remind him or her of what he or she does well.

The second vignette occurred during the third year of our program when one of the afterschool teachers called me and said, "We have a problem." The school's test-prep tutoring classes had started and all at-risk students were strongly urged to attend these sessions for two afternoons a week until the test in late April. Of our 15 afterschool students, 10 were considered at-risk. This left the staff with the dilemma of either selecting only those students from classrooms considered for the "gifted," or trying to convince the parents of the at-risk students to keep their children out of the test-prep tutoring classes after school so that they might still attend the *In Addition* program. The staff considered neither option appropriate. The *In Addition* program was not designated solely for children labeled gifted or at-risk. Indeed the staff worked actively to mitigate these discriminatory labels. The project was open to all who wished to participate and was limited only by group size. Likewise, the staff did not feel they could urge parents to keep their children out of test-prep classes because the *In Addition* program did not directly provide skill practice and review. The staff understood why parents would want their children to receive any assistance that might increase their children's chances for success in taking the high-stakes tests.

The staff spoke with the school principal to enlist his help in solving our dilemma.

He agreed to work with them. They immediately called an emergency meeting with all stakeholders: parents, *In Addition* students, the principal, the *In Addition* teacher, and the *In Addition* staff, composed of the director, researcher, videographer, and curriculum advisor. The staff presented a possible solution: if the parents would take on the role of test-prep teachers for their children the staff would provide them with the materials that they would need to tutor at home in the evening or on weekends. This would mean that parents would undertake a major responsibility, but the staff committed themselves to helping parents accomplish this. Parents were asked to consider the proposal for a week. During the next meeting the parents reported that they had decided to take on the challenge, in spite of their often very hectic lives and the fact that some parents were working two jobs.

The *In Addition* staff purchased the materials and held work meetings every three weeks in order to help parents learn the mathematics they needed to assist their children. Dinner was provided for the parents so they wouldn't have to cook a meal for the family when they returned home later that night. During these meetings the staff hired a graduate student to provide homework help for the children while they did their homework and ate pizza.

The result of this story is brief, but amazing. Every student participating in the *In Addition* afterschool program passed the test. The staff makes no claims about whether parent intervention was responsible or if attendance in the afterschool program helped students to perform well on the tests. What we do know is that students did not have to spend afterschool hours drilling and memorizing math facts in order to be successful on test-taking day.

ADVICE FROM A TEACHER

I asked a good friend of mine who has been teaching for several years what she does to prepare her students for taking standardized tests. This is her e-mail response to my question:

> I would like to be arrogant and say that good teaching should be preparation enough for the test but there are some things I do in my students' best interest. We practice released questions from previous years so I can be sure the students are familiar with the look of the question they will face. I begin with easy questions to build confidence and elicit comments like, "Hey, this isn't so hard." The biggest thing is problem-solving strategies. I think it is imperative to help students develop an automatic procedure for solving problems. This is what Cheryl, another teacher in my grade level, and I have been working on with our games. Identify the problem, or "What question are they asking you? What numbers are necessary to solve the problem? What operation will you use?" And then above all check your answer, use your common sense, and ask yourself, "Does this answer make sense given the question or problem?"
>
> I find this to be a major weakness of the forced calculation kids have had to endure—even my fifth graders have stopped thinking. My goal is to get them to be good thinkers.

SUPPORTING RESEARCH

I recently read an article by Thomas O'Brien and Christine Wallach (2006) about a study designed to examine how groups of fifth-grade students from three different classrooms engaged in a challenge problem requiring inference and logical thinking. Each of the classrooms embraced different teaching and learning philosophies. Three groups of children participated. The students in group 1 were from a middle-class private school in a major city where the school's approach was "teaching for understanding" and textbooks were rarely used for instruction. Group 2 was made up of fifth graders from a private suburban school and the curriculum was provided by a textbook series. Group 3 was from an urban school where memorization was the method of teaching.

Each group was given the following challenge: four or more children form a circle in front of the class and the teacher secretly identifies a student as the mystery person and writes down that person's name. The rules of the game *game* are for the rest of the class to figure out who the mystery person is by asking questions. If the mystery person is named, the teacher responds with "hot." If the person is seated next to the mystery person the teacher also responds with "hot." All other responses are "cold."

The results were amazing. Group 1 was able to use inferences and met the challenge with eagerness. This is a tribute to the teachers' willingness to teach beyond the test and challenge students to think on a more sophisticated level. Group 2 viewed teacher responses as isolated bits of information, failed to see relationships between pieces of data, and lacked overall comprehension of the problem. Group 3 had no success at determining the mystery person. They did not understand what the problem entailed or how to logically approach a solution. The message I gained from reading this study is that how we teach has a huge influence on how students think. If our expectations are that children think, solve problems, and look for new problems and questions we might be closer to group 1's experience. Allowing a textbook alone to dominate our mathematics teaching will limit our students to sound bytes of math knowledge and limit their ability to problem solve and transfer their understandings in successful ways to new problems and situations. If memorization is equated with learning we are crippling our students to rely on unrelated pieces of information and severely disabling their ability to think critically in novel situations.

ONE STUDENT'S ASSESSMENT EXPERIENCE

One assignment in an inquiries course, a required course for every education major at the university, is to write a vignette that is either a positive or negative perspective of a time when you were assessed. The following paper written by Rob Cohen, sums up this chapter.

Nearly every college student in this country faces the same assessment: the SAT. The test is decidedly not an intelligence test, so its purposes remain vague. The SAT supposedly measures aptitude, an intrinsically unquantifiable characteristic. One could—and many do—argue that the SAT simply measures a student's aptitude to take the SAT.

In Rose Tree Media School District students learn about the SAT firsthand in the seventh grade. Whether or not anybody admitted it outright, everybody saw the SAT as a measure of intellectual potential to some extent. We took the test, got confused, got our scores, and got more confused. Hence my introduction to the "most important test of my life" did little more than frighten me that I had finally encountered an academic obstacle that I could not overcome.

By the time I finished my freshman year of high school I had reached an academic stride. I was near the top of my class, and I had become intellectually engaged by most of the material in school (with or without the teacher's help, depending on the class). With this confidence I took the SAT (or PSAT—I don't even remember) my sophomore year of high school. The score I eventually received did not end up reflecting the academic greatness that I had thought I embodied. It was not a bad score by any means, but it was an average score. It was not a "great" score, and I was a "great" student.

I soon began to realize, as junior and senior year rolled around, that this test might present more than just a small annoyance to me. Now in college-prep mode, I had begun to look at myself as a college admissions board might. My grades and class rank were superb, I looked well rounded and passionate on paper as well as in person, and I could present myself well, but I had still had this mediocre skeleton in the closet (that unfortunately could not stay there) with the SAT. My rebellious adolescent mind no longer took any stock in the worth of the test's verdict. However, agree with it or not, I still had to do well on the damned thing.

By senior year, all of the college-bound students were buzzing with preparations and last-minute improvements in the hopes of getting into their dream schools. I had finally found mine. As I had secured the last of my teacher recommendations and put the finishing touches on a splendid personal statement, I also received my final SAT score: a 1290. This was the bottom range of the average scores that Wesleyan accepted, so I was just satisfied enough not to be livid. I sent off my early-decision application and waited.

Coming home from school in December, I got my first word from Wesleyan: deferred. Many tears of frustration and anger followed. I was furious that I had probably wasted all of the time and hard work that I had put into school. I thought about all of the stupid assignments and tests that I had prepared for—completely devoid of any valuable learning—just to receive a letter grade, just "to get into a 'good' school." I could have spent that time working on music or not working at all.

I had the choice to send my application through a second early-decision process or apply regularly in the spring. Again I applied early-decision and waited. In the spring I was finally accepted, but I was left grimacing with the bitter taste of the SAT and of the college admissions process in general. As I excelled in college and witnessed mass stupidity on the part of my peers more often than not, I sometimes thought back to my "aptitude" test and Wesleyan's admissions test with a bittersweet sense of victory.

TO SUM IT UP

Standardized testing has its purposes, and one function is to quantify learning experiences across classrooms, districts, and states in an effort to ensure equal learning opportunity for all students. Standardized tests were not intended to be used as an evaluation tool for teachers, parents, and students about a particular student's progress, what she knows and doesn't know, or how a teacher might meet those individual needs. Assessments that are closer to the action of the classroom—such as portfolios, individual teacher tests, self-assessments, parental input, and teacher observations—all provide valuable insights into a student's learning and progress. Yet, in today's accountability environment standardized tests are being used to make life-altering decisions about students, teachers, and schools and, therefore, cannot be ignored. Finding the appropriate balance between preparing students to take the standardized tests and assisting students in being more responsible for their own learning assessments is a difficult challenge. The challenge is worth the fight. If we roll over and play dead to the real issue at stake in all this, which is valuing learning over memorizing facts and procedures, then everyone loses the school game. Also the likelihood that students will find joy in learning as adults or that they will critically engage in their world with discrimination and mindful inquiry is much diminished.

TEACHER AS RESEARCHER THOUGHTS

1. I encourage each of you to write your own observations of students and your classroom on test day. Just write what you observe and hear.

2. It may be empowering to interview students about their own thoughts about testing. This could be accomplished individually or as a small focus group of five or six students. Keep the questions neutral and limited in number. Let the students direct the flow of the discussion: "In a few weeks we will be taking the math test. What are your thoughts as the day approaches?"

3. Choose a single topic in the curriculum and commit to using a project approach rather than using direct instruction. For example, if you provide a variety of experiences for students to explore properties of area and perimeter but never have a formal lesson dealing with how to find the area and perimeter of objects, record student performance on any test questions that address area and perimeter. You might do this on your own or as a schoolwide project to look at various teaching strategies. If individual student test results are not made available, give a practice exam on your own.

Chapter 7

How Can We Take Critical Thinking
Beyond the Classroom?

Whole School Projects: The Bigger Picture

When the entire school shares a math focus it is noticeable the moment you walk through the front doors of the school. I speak from experience, as I was a research associate for an evaluation of a national K–2 math specialist project that took me to several school districts across the country. I would visit several schools in a single district and interview parents, students, teachers, and administrators to gather data about the project from the perspectives of the various project stakeholders. It was on the second day of a visit to a large urban school district on the west coast that I was able to differentiate clearly between a school that does interesting mathematics and one that has a whole school mathematics focus. The distinction was unmistakable as I entered the front door of Walker Elementary School and immediately noticed a large hand-drawn map on the wall next to the door. After walking over to look more closely at the map, it became clear that this was a scale drawing of the neighborhood. On the map were colored stickers that designated student homes. Next to the map were students' first names and next to each name was a distance from home to school recorded in a variety of ways. For example, Eileen lived 10 minutes by bicycle from the school while Anthony lived 1,573 steps away.

As I continued my walk through the corridors toward the principal's office, I was astounded to see bar graphs hanging on every inch of wall space. Some of the graph titles included "How Many Pets?" "Our Favorite Sports," and "Which Story Would You Recommend?" I saw a line graph with "Distances to School Places." Students had measured in feet and yards how far to the library, the cafeteria, the gym, the office, and the art room.

Outside a third-grade classroom was a Venn diagram with fields labeled *James and the Giant Peach* and *Cricket in Times Square.*

As I passed a fourth-grade classroom I noticed large, life-size figures of people with measurement labels on them. I stopped at one called "Measurement Morris" and read the assignment posted to the left. The directions had been to draw a person who was 56 inches tall, with arms 15 inches in length. The shirt should have three 1-inch buttons and stripes that were each ½-inch wide. The cuffs on the pants should each measure 2 inches. The "person" could be named or enhanced with any additional details the group wanted to add to make him or her unique.

Such a coordinated effort at building mathematics competency across all grades sends a powerful message to children, parents, and visitors alike. Math is valued here. Students are engaged in learning mathematics that is relevant to their lives. Mathematics is perceived to be something that may be done in collaboration with others. The notion of a whole school effort taking shape may seem overwhelming. However, think about beginning with a grade-level project and move toward an extension to the whole school after experiencing the success of efforts in planning a smaller scope of math coordination.

HOW FAR AROUND OUR SCHOOL?

When I taught fourth grade my team teaching partner and I challenged our students to estimate the length of our classroom. After much discussion and a range of measurement estimations, the students calculated the length of the room. Many strategies were used. The ruler-to-ruler approach, placing a piece of string the length of the room and then measuring the string, and determining a length of unifix cubes that was equal to 10 inches and then counting by 10s were some of the ways students solved the task of measuring the room's length. This led to the next task—to gauge the length of the hallway from our class, which was at the far east wing of the building, to the kindergarten, which was located on the far west wing. Students eagerly began to strategize ways to find the answer to this challenge and worked collaboratively in their groups to reach a solution. They worked on this problem for several days, and at the end of the week the whole class convened for a "measurement meeting" in which individual groups shared their solutions in a lively discussion. Students had taken ownership of their work and were therefore eager to participate and question each other.

Students were then given this question: What is the distance around our school? Again, they worked together to come up with a strategy to get the answer. One group's strategy in the previous problem of finding the distance from one end of the school building to the other was to assess the distance of one person with outstretched arms and then use that information to calculate the distance they could measure using all the students in the class. Of course this wasn't even close to the number of armlengths they were going to need to measure around the school, as the students discovered after a trip outside to mark off how far around the school they extended. Students then asked if they could get other classrooms involved. After getting approval from their teachers, they formed a committee to meet with Mr. Smith, the principal. On Tuesday the newly formed committee met with Mr. Smith to ask if he would assist them in enlisting the help of the whole school to measure the perimeter of the school building. Mr. Smith said he thought it was a fine idea and suggested that the end of the second lunch period would be the beginning of lunch for one-third of the students. He would ask the kindergarten teachers if they would agree to join us at that time as well. The whole plan was scheduled to take place on Thursday. Students were animated and decided to call the local newspaper to take pictures of the measurement event. They also placed a ballot box in the cafeteria and library for classmates in all grades to guess the distance around the school.

The day was a huge success. It took much more organization than the students had originally anticipated. Getting everyone outside and explaining how to extend arm to arm in a line around the building necessitated two students from our class to assist each class of students from other grades. There were not enough students to reach around the building so students placed markers at the beginning and ending spots and after everyone returned to lunch and classes our students used themselves to finish the measurement of the distance around the school—starting from the previously placed markers. On Friday morning students made an announcement to the whole school to report their results and announced the winners of the estimation challenge.

One Hundredth Day

A practice that has become commonplace in many elementary schools is a Hundredth Day Celebration. Students begin counting each day they attend school and learn place value concepts in the process by using a popsicle stick to represent each day. After 10 days, students group the 10 sticks or color the number 10 on the calendar or hundredths chart with a different color. Students learn to count by 10s and start to notice number patterns. Throughout the days and months students learn how to skip count, locate missing numbers, and understand the concepts of more/less, before/after, and base 10. After 100 days of school, students celebrate 100 with a variety of activities that extend throughout the grades. For more ideas on One Hundredth Day activities, read *Math Their Way* by Mary Baratta-Lorton (1976) or the article "Math Journals Boost Real Learning" (Burns & Silbey, 2001).

RECESS

How many times in the typical adult workday are adults expected to sit and diligently work at a desk for intervals of over 6 or 7 hours during which talking with colleagues about any topic other than work is not allowed, and where the only break in the day is one taken for a 45-minute lunch? As strange as it may seem this is the expectation we place on many schoolchildren, an expectation that as adults we would deem demeaning and restrictive. Accountability and time-on-task is driving this shift away from recess time to more time for instruction, even though research clearly shows that student attention decreases the longer students go without a break (Pelligrini & Bohn, 2005, p. 13) and that attention increases immediately after recess.

Recess is the single time of the day when many students are free to socialize on their own terms, without rules, tasks to be completed, and companions chosen. The skills students learn in the process of being social actually help them learn and do not detract from learning. Allowing students to navigate such socially complicated problems as how to get invited to play, choose teams, take turns, cope with losing and winning, decide what game to play, whom to play with, or overcome feeling incompetent—these are all problem-solving skills that will translate to children not only being more adept social beings, but also better learners.

As a teacher, I found recess the perfect opportunity to observe students informally and to make assessment notes about their choices and demeanors during unstructured times with their peers. It was often the students who were able to solve recess situations on their own or with peers and without teacher intervention. These were also the students who often met math challenges with confidence. Problem solving requires a sense of "I can figure this out" rather than a reaction to problems with "Let's ask the teacher" or "Is this right?" Recess is the perfect venue in which to trust students to spend their free time engaged in an activity that brings them some pleasure, to believe that students need time to make decisions for themselves and that giving them this trust will also strengthen their learning achievement. Teachers may want to read *The Recess Queen* by Alexis O'Neill (2002) and *Recess Pieces* by Bob Fingerman (2006) to the students as a means of opening up discussion about recess and problem solving during unstructured time.

AFTERSCHOOL MATH PROGRAM

Throughout this book there are references regarding mathematics learning that takes place in an afterschool program called *In Addition*. This program reenvisions afterschool math by seeking to engage children in learning by encouraging them to ask their own real-life questions. The National Council of Teachers of Mathematics (NCTM, 2000) posits that mathematical understanding increases when students are engaged in real-life, problem-based learning. The National Research Council (NRC, 2001) recommends providing students with opportunities to investigate ideas collaboratively as a community of learners in order to discover multiple strategies that lead to a deeper understanding of mathematics. Collaborative questioning and conversations can also contribute to a sense of shared learning that reduces the competitive inclinations often associated with a traditional learning environment. Steven Levy, the author of *Starting From Scratch* (1996), suggests, "Asking questions promotes an interest in the 'Other,' acting as a balance to the self-absorption and the self-centeredness that so pervades our culture" (p. 37).

In Addition **Rationale**

Many elementary schools are not afforded such learning "luxury." "Surveys of U.S. teachers have consistently shown that nearly all their instructional time is structured around textbooks or other commercially produced materials, even though teachers vary substantially in the extent to which they follow a book's organization and suggested activities" (NRC, 2001, p. 36). In responding to a 1996 National Assessment of Educational Progress (NAEP) mathematics assessment, teachers reported that fourth graders were usually tested in mathematics once or twice a month. About one-third of the children took tests once or twice a week, even though more frequent testing was associated with lower achievement (NRC, 2001, p. 40). Over 90% of these teachers reported that they gave considerable emphasis to facts, concepts, skills, and procedures; only 52% focused on reasoning processes and even fewer, 30%, on communication.

Often teachers explain the disparity between mathematics reform goals and the realities of the classroom as "not having enough time" to help students discover mathematics. Sometimes curriculum and testing pressures, fueled by an ever-increasing mantra of accountability based on standardized tests (Eisner, 2003), place rigid teaching and learning expectations on teachers and students. While rigid adherence to curriculum is meant to help students achieve higher test scores, national results show that this emphasis is not working (Eisner, 2003). The cost, moreover, is a loss of joy about learning mathematics that not only decreases learning potential but also produces mathematics anxiety and frequently leaves students with a view that mathematics is a discrete set of skills with no relevance to their lives. Mathematics learning then becomes rote and compliant memorization of facts and procedures in which students merely plug in a formula to get the desired answer to an isolated, irrelevant question.

Beliefs about how children learn provided the theoretical framework on which the three *In Addition* afterschool learning principles were identified:

1. Children learn when they are engaged and fascinated. Encouraging children to explore things they wonder about and to think about new questions creates a cycle of excitement. Instead of being drudgery, learning becomes an enjoyable, satisfying experience that begs to be repeated over and over again in a variety of new circumstances (Dewey, 1938/1963).

2. Children learn when they share their ideas and thinking with others in a community of learning. Building urban learning communities of trust (Ennis & McCauley, 2002; Wayne, 2002) leads to socially and experientially constructed learning that enhances people's ability to discuss ideas, develop reasoning capabilities, and establish a habit of collaborative problem posing and solving. A learning environment in which respect for the thinking of all is the norm allows students to think about things from new perspectives.

3. Children learn when their learning is embedded in themselves, their homes, and their communities. By assisting students to seek pathways of discovery for their curiosities, we equip them to bridge their school mathematics learning to their lives outside school. Helping students to look at their neighborhoods to ask questions about what they see and know provides a social life for knowledge and meaning making as an ongoing, collaborative process.

Program Context and Design

In Addition is situated in an elementary school in New York City. In early September flyers are distributed to every student in grades 3, 4, and 5 inviting them to consider participation in the *In Addition* afterschool program. Students are randomly selected from the returned flyers through a lottery system, taking 10 students each from the third, fourth, and fifth grades to comprise two *In Addition* groups of 15 students each. Opportunity to participate is not limited to distinct populations such as gifted or at-risk students because a goal of *In Addition* is to ensure a heterogeneous learning environment. The only criterion for acceptance was a commitment to attend two hours a day, three days a week, from September to May.

The *In Addition* project team is comprised of an assistant professor of mathematics education, two New York City classroom teachers who teach the afterschool program in their own classrooms from 3:30 to 5:30, a research professor, and a research consultant. Combining the recommendations of the NRC and the NCTM, the *In Addition* afterschool program aims to facilitate the teaching and learning of mathematics outside of such classroom constraints as high-stakes testing and grades. Although basic math skills are important, these skills are developed through providing students opportunities to learn mathematics when the motivation to learn comes from within; when the quest to satisfy curiosity is honored; when ideas can evolve and percolate and bring forth insight, wonder, and understanding; when everyone—children, teachers, parents, and community members—is involved. Students' questions and interests guide learning investigations linked to their neighborhood. Students help each other become more aware of and connected to their community by examining their world through the lenses of their diverse backgrounds. Parent participation, through workshops and retreats, provides both a support system for students and links among home, school, and community.

ADOPT A CAUSE

An example of one project undertaken by the students of one *In Addition* after-school group is the animal shelter project. After a visit to the local shelter, the *In Addition* afterschool program wanted to do something to support the work of the pet adoption program. The students brainstormed ways to raise money to donate to the shelter to help pay for the food and medical shots needed to keep the dogs and cats healthy while awaiting adoption. Recently, students had read *Sadako and the Thousand Paper Cranes* by Eleanor Coerr in their classes. The suggestion was made to make paper cranes and sell them at the parent meeting and open house scheduled for later in the month. The *In Addition* teacher provided origami paper for the students to try making paper cranes. After many attempts and much frustration students learned how to fold the paper with ease and calculated it took an average of 8 minutes to complete a paper crane. They did the mathematics and discovered that if each of the 15 *In Addition* students made 10 paper cranes and they sold them for $2 each they could raise $300 to give to the animal shelter.

Students set about completing the designated number of paper cranes by the week's end. They set up a table at the entrance to the meeting room the evening of the parent meeting and demonstrated how to make the cranes. Students also made a poster with facts and quotes from the director of the animal shelter. The poster presentation included a graph with their goal of $300 and it was colored in as cranes were sold. Parents purchased 67 cranes with a net gain of $142. Six parents paid $5 each for their cranes.

But how were they to sell the remaining cranes in order to reach the goal of $300? Students came up with a new marketing approach. They added colorful embroidery thread to make the cranes hanging ornaments and designed a small brochure explaining that the proceeds would support the neighborhood animal shelter. Each afterschool student took five of the cranes with brochures and gave them to neighbors, friends, and family members. All but 3 of the 75 cranes students gave out were sold. This brought the total to $288. The goal was in sight. The *In Addition* teacher asked if they had asked the people in the office to buy any cranes. Students quickly headed for the office and sold the remaining eight paper cranes for $22. The secretary paid $10 for two and the principal, the assistant principal, and the parent coordinator each bought two for $2 a piece.

Students were so excited on the following Tuesday to visit the animal shelter and proudly present the director with $310. The director was astounded at the work the students had done on the shelter's behalf and told the children it was efforts such as theirs that would help the animal shelter to continue its work with lost and abandoned dogs and cats.

A second example of students taking on a cause comes from a New York City fifth-grade teacher who asked her students to consider ways they might "give back" to the community. Students' initial suggestions included helping the homeless and planting flowers in the neighborhood. After a longer discussion students decided to visit the senior care facility that was on the same block as the school. Students each found a sponsor to support their efforts and with the money collected from the sponsoring adults, their teacher purchased cards, read-aloud books, and math games to bring with them when they visited the senior care facility. During the visits the students paired with small groups of seniors and played games such as cribbage, Set, and dominoes. Before leaving, the students read stories to the seniors. The games and books were donated to the facility for use during future visits and for use by the seniors between visits.

INTERDISCIPLINARY OPPORTUNITIES

More often than not mathematics is perceived as a discrete discipline without relevance in other learning areas. The truth is, mathematics is the easiest of content areas to integrate into other content areas. The reason for this is that math is a part of every aspect of our lives, all that we do—from measurement, design, architecture, reason and proof, and rhythm, to the sports we play. In the following paragraphs I illustrate ways that math might be woven into other content areas.

The School Library

A timeline that reaches around the library within reach of all students is a way to help students make connections between the different time frames of the books they are reading and would enable them to see where they are situated in historical contexts. For older students, seeing *October Sky* by Homer Hickam (1999) on the timeline in close proximity to the first U.S. astronaut in space and in relation to the more recent discovery, almost 40 years later, of Pluto no longer being designated a planet allows students to visualize the story they are reading in relation to other major historical events. Younger children take delight in noting such dates as the year their school was built and the years in which favorite authors, such as A. A. Milne or Eric Carle, wrote their first books.

The library catalog system is mathematical. A study of how books are categorized and how to find a book based on this mathematical system enhances a student's grasp of sorting and classifying beyond the basic scientific model. Sorting and classifying is the basis of all reasoning and the way we all make sense of our worlds. The library classification structure stretches the way students think about this important skill.

As children begin to use a library, they gradually learn that the books there are arranged so that those that are similar are grouped together. Because they usually start browsing first in the picture book section, they may become aware that the books have spine labels with letters on them, and that those letters are arranged alphabetically by the last names of authors. As they grow older, however, and move around the library looking for books that match their changing interests—on dinosaurs, drawing, outer space, caring for pets—they may also become aware that many of these books have numbers on their spine labels, and that books on the same subject have similar numbers. But who decides what these numbers should be? And how does it happen that in almost all school and public libraries books about the history of the United States will have the number of 973, and books about the myths of ancient Greece will have the number 292?

Librarians and media specialists usually teach children about how the library is arranged gradually through the grades. By the time children are in the third grade they have usually discussed differences between story books (the picture book and fiction sections) and books we read for information (the nonfiction sections). Your media specialist may display a map of the library with the various sections labeled. And there may be a chart in your library with the title "Dewey Decimal System" and a list of the ten categories identified by their numbers from 001 to 099 up to 900 to 999:

001–099	Generalities (encyclopedias, almanacs, etc.)
100–199	Philosophy and psychology
200–299	Religion and mythology
300–399	Social sciences (civics, law, economics, customs, etc.)
400–499	Languages
500–599	Pure sciences (mathematics, astronomy, biology, etc.)
600–699	Applied sciences (medicine, engineering, agriculture, etc.)
700–799	Fine arts
800–899	Literature
900–999	Geography and history

If there is no media specialist in the school, the teacher may assign children to find out where those numbers came from and what they mean. A clue for such an assignment could well be "Find out who Melvil Dewey was and why he is important to us. Most of us have never heard his name, but he invented something we use almost every day." An article in the *World Book* encyclopedia will tell students that Melvil Dewey (1851–1931) devised what has come to be called the Dewey Decimal System, in which all knowledge would be divided into 10 main classes. As a young man Dewey worked as a librarian in the Amherst College Library. In those days books were usually arranged by color or size, and he decided to invent a system in which they could be arranged by subject.

The 10 main classes Dewey first devised had to be subdivided further to accommodate all the books on so many subjects, and so the "decimal" parts of the classification numbers were developed. The large numbers are all broken down into smaller subjects. For example, in the 600s, agriculture is placed in 630–639; useful insects are put in 638; beekeeping is given the number 638.1; and silkworms are 638.2.

Many media specialists work collaboratively with classroom teachers to integrate their lessons on library arrangement with teacher assignments for research reports or for independent reading. Before the actual assignment begins, children can be introduced to a new curriculum unit with a class activity to "find their mystery books" by looking for an assigned number or numbers and bringing back to their tables groups of books on the coming unit, whether it be insects, planets, or land biomes of the world.

Students have difficulty locating or putting away books subdivided by decimal numbers until they understand how the decimal system works. At that point, the librarian will want to introduce new lessons that lead students to look for books with more lengthy decimal numbers and subjects with more subdivisions. Teachers may also want to coordinate a visit to the local public library—perhaps based on a curriculum unit in science or social studies—that will help students become more aware that the arrangement by the same Dewey decimal numbers (usually referred to as "call numbers") is used there also.

The Gym Class

Physical education is laden with mathematical connections. Measurements of different sport spaces—football field, basketball court, Olympic swimming pool, or the running track—all offer math tasks or comparisons for students to explore. The height of the tennis net and the weight of a baseball bat, the angle of a baseball pitch, the statistics of any sport team, and the time a runner finishes a marathon are all mathematics-rich learning opportunities that also provide heightened motivation for students. Talk with children and ask what interests them—sports will be at the top of most lists.

Music

The beats of popular songs provide an easy-to-understand fraction lesson for students of any age. Dance steps and clapping to the beats of songs help to build pattern recognition and fractional intervals with younger children. Most music teachers would be happy to coordinate a lesson on the meaning of 3/4, 4/4, or 6/8 on music staffs with your lesson on fractions for intermediate grades.

I recently was introduced to Sharon Roffman, who founded ClassNotes, a nonprofit organization committed to working with teachers and students to integrate music education into the academic curriculum. The following description is taken from the ClassNotes Web site:

> For example, on "math day" a fifth grade class studying fractions might be introduced to a Bela Bartok string quartet. Using their knowledge of fractions, the students would learn to decipher the quartet's complicated rhythms. In the end, the students have a better understanding of the math concept and its practical implications, and they may have also become acquainted with the Bartok quartet. Teachers who might otherwise be hesitant to give up valuable teaching time appreciate that the lessons actually reinforce the very concepts they are teaching. (http://www.classnotesinfo.org/pictures.php)

Art

Tessellation is a perfect example of art and math intertwined. For any student, a study of M. C. Escher's work offers an obvious mathematical perspective to art and design. Younger students can explore his work and talk about what they notice. They can create simple cut-and-replace designs that, when repeated, tessellate and make a pattern. Older students can make much more elaborate tessellation designs that make use of geometric flips, slides, and rotations.

Social Studies

I recently read an article published in *The Council Chronicle* (Aronson, 2006) that highlights a perfect example of mathematics integration with the social studies curriculum. Deb Aronson reported how a school used a study of the First Amendment as a powerful tool to teach critical thinking. Students demonstrated their understanding of the First Amendment in a variety of ways after an opinion poll conducted by the BBC revealed few adults even knew what the

First Amendment was and after the Knight Foundation reported that three out of four students did not have any knowledge about the First Amendment. There are many civic issues/personalities in the elementary school curriculum that lend themselves to <u>fostering an environment of critical thinking:</u> flag burning, Rosa Parks, Columbus Day, United Nations, the world shortage of clean water, global warming, and Indian reservations.

Poetry

Poetry and mathematics may sound like disparate universes to many of you but I want to share some experiences I have had with both reading math poetry and having students create poems about math content. Theoni Pappas has a math poetry book for shared voices entitled *Math Talk: Mathematical Ideas in Poems for Two Voices* (1991) that I have cherished as a classroom resource. From time to time, often as a "change of pace" activity, I will ask for two volunteers to do a poetry reading for the class. These poems are filled with math language regarding every aspect of math content—such as numbers, geometry, division, and subtraction—and are written for two voices to read aloud. I have invited students to use their math journals to write about what they learned in a unit on triangles. Here is a sample of the poems written by students:

> Equilateral Triangle
> Three sides
>   all equal
> Three angles equal too
>   I measured, cut,
>   And with some glue
> An equilateral triangle
> Just for you.
>   Obtuse Triangle
>   Looks like it's falling over
>   But it isn't
>   One angle bigger than the other two
>   Not tipping, just obtuse.

The structure of traditional poetic forms is highly mathematical and allows students to explore syllable and the pattern recognition of 5, 7, 5 found in the haiku form. Older students can learn the meaning of iambic pentameter or the mathematics underlying sonnet form. Students may also experiment with their own forms and create poems with a 7, 11, 7 or a 5, 3, 5 pattern. After a study of the Fibonacci sequence (1, 1, 2, 3, 5, 8, 13, 21, etc.), students may want to try to create poems in the same form. It is, after all, found in many other places in nature—why not in our poetic expressions?

Any and all of these integrated ideas would lend themselves to a "Hallway Math Gallery." A whole school math theme would be evident to parents, students, teachers, and visitors as they walk through the halls seeing graphs, drawings, timelines, poetry, and music fractions displayed.

COMMUNITY OUTREACH: VISITS TO LOCAL BUSINESSES

A whole school focus on mathematics sends a clear, undeniable message—that math is valued. Taking this commitment to mathematics learning beyond the parking lot of the school and reaching out to the community communicates the mission to a broader audience:

- To the community: come see what we are teaching and learning in our classrooms.
- To the businesspeople in the community: what you do as businesspeople in our community can help our students learn mathematics.
- To students: math is a life skill, one that is necessary for any profession.

Visits to Local Businesses

Designate a community math month where every grade level visits a different local business and talks with the people who work there about the math they use in their daily jobs. This can be followed up with math-related classroom activities. The following are shared as possibilities to demonstrate how learning goes both ways.

First Grade Goes to the Post Office

Prior to the visit to the post office, students collect letters and packages that have been received in their homes and bring them into class for examination and discovery. Have students sort them, look for similarities and differences, and notice the stamps. You could map the locations from where they originated on a large map.

During the post office visit they can learn how sorting and classifying are used to keep the mail delivery efficient and how scales determine the price of stamps and package mailing costs. How many letters pass through the post office each day will be an opportunity to think about large numbers in a real-life context.

Back in the classroom, students can set up their own post office and mail letters to each other. Have them design a system for sorting the mail received and create a route for delivery of the letters. Ask students to send letters to businesses in all 50 states asking for information and graph the return responses.

Second Grade Eats Out

A visit to a neighborhood restaurant is always a welcome field trip for any student. There are unlimited math areas to explore—the cost of items on the menu; the arrangement of tables and number of customers that can eat at the same time; bills that include tips, taxes, and change; graphing who comes to the restaurant and what they order; and itemizing the preparation of meals that includes quantities ordered and recipe amounts to accommodate large numbers of diners. Students might interview the owner, a chef, or a waitress to hear their individual math histories. In what ways do they use math in their jobs? What math did they learn in school that helps them? What math would they like to learn more about?

After they return to the classroom, in small groups of four, students can create a business plan for a restaurant of their own design. The plan must include:

- A name
- A menu
- A seating plan

Students might send out surveys to every student in the school asking what their favorite restaurant food is and then represent the results in a graph to hang in the hall. If you have parent helpers or want to make this a more elaborate project, students might create a classroom restaurant for a week and offer simple choices of soup and sandwiches for teachers and other adults in the school.

Third-Grade Patchwork: A Visit to the Quilt Shop

If your community has a quilt shop this is tailor-made for math learning. Share a few children's literature books about quilts prior to visiting the shop. Some possible selections might consist of *Eight Hands Round* by Ann Whitford Paul, which illustrates several quilt designs and explains the historical significance of each pattern, *The Patchwork Quilt* by Valerie Flournoy, which is a Coretta Scott King Award–winning book that brings forth the personal connections and meaning of quilts and is a celebration of family. If your school has a budget for project learning, you might consider having students design a class quilt. Students have to make decisions about the size of each square, shape of the pieces, color scheme for the quilt, and the pattern. During the visit to the quilt shop they can talk with the shop owner or some quilters to help them make these decisions.

Back in the classroom students create the individual quilt squares and with the help of a parent volunteer, sew together the separate quilt pieces to form one large quilt. Fractions lessons are a natural mathematics fit for quilting— what fractional part of the quilt is triangular in shape? What fractional part of the quilt is the red pattern cloth? Can you design a quilt that is ⅛ blue, ¼ red, and ½ yellow? Geoboards lend themselves to building skill with fractional understanding and quilt square design.

Fourth Grade Adopts the Animal Shelter

This project was explained earlier in the chapter. As a follow-up to the visit students might each adopt an imaginary cat or dog and design a pet house that they draw to scale. Students can also make a budget for caring for their pet for a year.

Fifth-Grade Movie Theater Study

A group of the *In Addition* afterschool students became interested in the local movie theater. Students wanted to know about the population of people who went to afternoon movies, which foods were the most popular at the concession stand, and how the movie image got to the screen. The kinds of questions will vary depending on the interests of your students, but it is a location that provides a wide range of topics to be explored in a single place.

After students gather initial data from their visit they can decide on the best way to represent the information they learned. Students may want to make a snack and sell it to other students at lunchtime, they may be eager to create their own short film, or decide to poll the school student body about their favorite films. Data gathering and graphing are important life skills and are often not given the attention in elementary school classrooms that will enable students to read "between the data" as well as reading the graph itself. More time in classrooms needs to be allotted to "what else do you want to know," "what doesn't the graph tell us," or "what does this information make you wonder about?" Typically, graph reading amounts to simple, lower-level questions such as, "How many more people go the movies at 5 p.m. than 3 p.m.?" Questions like this are merely basic computation and require very little critical thinking.

Town Hall Hosts the Sixth Grade

There is no place in a community where there is more mathematical information gathered together in one location than in the town hall. Records for everything—deaths, accidents, births, marriages, and pets—are all documented and open for public viewing. Plots and floor plans for homes, apartments, and subdivisions are also easily accessible and offer a multitude of math investigations.

Maps are the perfect venue to begin a study about neighborhood parks, building sites, or transportation.

As a fourth-grade teacher I collected old town reports from the town hall that dated back to the early 1900s. I gave each group of several students a collection of reports, making sure each group had one that dated back to the 1930s or 1940s with a report from the 1960s or 1970s and two more recent reports. Each group was asked to look through the documents and to decide as a group something to study. The students then made charts and from the charts made predictions for the years 2010 and 2030. Students were instructed to support their predictions with factual data that also included ratios and percentages.

This project was of high interest to the students—many related their study to personal connections such as grandparents who lived in the community back in the 1950s or to future plans about their own families in 20 years.

Community Math Celebration

To celebrate the community math learning that resulted from the activities and visits to local businesses during "math month," students, parents, and community members can plan for a math fair to be held as a culminating celebration. What needs to be considered in the planning are:

Who will attend?

What form of advertising will be used and who will fund the cost?

Will there be a fee for admission and, if so, what to do with the proceeds?

Will the celebration be held during the week or on a weekend?

What will be the participation of students, parents, and community businesspeople?

Will booths be shared or complementary? For example, will the quilt shop create its own booth or will it work with the students on a single booth about quilting?

Will there be some sort of product produced by individual booths or a product resulting from all the booths? What might that be?

MATH FAIR: EVERYONE IS INVITED

A friend of mine who teaches in Michigan told me about a math fair her school put on for parents. The theme of the fair was "Summertime in February" and every class in the school created games or booths representing this theme of sun, vacation, and water fun. Students from kindergarten to sixth grade worked on their projects for weeks. On the afternoon of the math fair students set up their interactive math games in the gym and by evening everyone sat waiting for the parents to attend. No one anticipated the attendance of so many

parents—15 classrooms participated and the attendance, not including students, tallied 327! The gym was transformed into a math amusement park with
booths, popcorn, prizes, and take-home games. Parents, siblings, and students
alike all enjoyed math together in a spirit of fun and sharing rarely associated
with math learning. The admission fee of $2.50 was used to purchase math
literature books for each grade.

Combining efforts and learning together bring incredible benefits for all
stakeholders in an endeavor such as this. Community members feel connected
to the schools in new ways, oftentimes uncovering a heretofore hidden sense of
responsibility for contributing to the growth and development of the youth in
the neighborhood. Local businesses can introduce new patrons to their place
of business through student interest and the parents of students. Students come
across fresh ideas and information regarding the community in which they
live. A visit to the town hall in sixth grade might possibly trigger an interest in
town politics or in a career as a land surveyor for a student.

THE COMMUNITY AS CURRICULUM

Steven Levy created a unique connection between school and community with
his "On the Bicycle Path" project (Levy, 1996). His fourth-grade students were
asked in the first week of school what the most significant events in their lives
were. He collected student responses on the blackboard and it was clear that
the construction of a bicycle path in the community was one event most of the
students mentioned. The class set out to organize the bicycle path as a focus for
learning during the year that would encompass all content areas in the curriculum. Students' mathematics learning centered on graphing data, measurement,
problem solving, and number sense and operations. Language arts learning
revolved around writing letters to community members asking about their
opinions 10 years after the path was constructed. Students also read articles
and reports written before, during, and after the path was built. As a culminating project the class wrote their own report about their findings and published
it. Social studies involved visiting town hall and as a result students came to
better understand the government processes that were involved in passing the
bicycle path bond issue. Students also attended town hall meetings and experienced government policy making firsthand. Science learning occurred when
students made a visit to the department of public works and learned how roads
were constructed and about the chemical changes that happen with differing
weather conditions. Community involvement was critical to this project, and
to recognize their contribution students invited the members of the community
who had participated in the project to the publication party and celebration at
the end of the year. Testimony from students, parents, and community members alike attest to the value of learning in our own backyards.

Why Reach Out?

Reaching out produces advantages we might overlook otherwise—supporting the notion that math is everywhere, building school community, and generating positive public relations with community. In our tightly structured curriculum, test-driven learning schedules can be easily pushed to the back burner.

Building School Community

Each school community is characterized by the relationship and communication patterns that exist among students and teachers and across grade levels. Is learning limited to individual classrooms or do students and teachers have opportunities to establish relationships beyond the immediate boundaries of the classroom? Can they learn in collaboration with others in order to transport different perspectives, attitudes, and judgments across the educational cultures of separate classrooms? When we carry ideas and thinking from one classroom or one teacher to another there is a greater possibility that new thinking can be considered and discussed. It is new thinking that keeps us from recycling old ideas and keeps us from becoming "stale" in our opinions and wisdom.

Positive Community Relations

There is a great deal of wisdom in the saying "It takes a village to raise a child." Nothing but good can result from developing good relations with the community in which the school is situated. The more the school and community feel a tie of belonging to the other, the healthier both become. Students feel safe in places where they are known and where people care about their well-being. Community members may feel their tax dollars are well spent if they better understand the nature of the learning they are supporting.

CRITICAL THINKING: A WHOLE SCHOOL APPROACH

Teachers cannot infuse mathematics reasoning and critical thinking into every crevice of the school day without the help of a supportive administration. John Anzul is a principal of an elementary school whose "authentic voice" wholeheartedly endorses the concept of teachers and students moving beyond their own classrooms and bringing learning to the wider school environment and beyond. Surely John's sincere encouragement and advocacy played a large part in the enthusiastic teacher and student collaboration, which he describes next.

Dear Dr. McVarish:

After our recent conversation regarding the integration of math skills throughout the curriculum I wanted to follow up by telling you a little more about what we are currently doing at my school. For the past couple of years my staff and I have engaged in a series of discussions about how we could address math concepts in as many diverse ways as possible. In fact, at the start of this current year, for our site-based objective, we took on the challenge of improving math communications skills in all grade levels. We find that holding frequent conversations with students about how they solve problems improves their critical thinking skills in all curricular areas. Our students are often challenged to find alternative ways of solving the same problem, which also improves their skills in creative, critical thinking. Working together and talking to their peers about math is another way that students not only learn from their peers, but also learn to work cooperatively.

One specific schoolwide activity that recently took place may serve as an example of how we are integrating math skills across the curriculum. The new film version of the novel *Charlotte's Web* was scheduled to begin showing in the week before our holiday break. My second-grade teachers approached me with the idea of having our entire school attend the film as a large group. I asked them to present the idea at our next faculty meeting, and as more and more teachers began discussing the plan the details started to take shape. Since all teachers would have to collect money for admission the first- and second-grade teachers decided that letting the students assist would be a good way to let them practice counting money. Kindergarten teachers found numerous calendar activities as they shared portions of the story of seasons passing on a farm. Teachers quickly discovered that publishers of the novel were promoting the film by encouraging students to help them set a new record for the *Guinness Book of World Records*, which was for the most people reading the same passage aloud at the same time.

Students became increasingly excited as the days counted down to the event. The official Web site had a running clock that allowed them to practice telling time and tracking elapsed time. There was also a running tally of participants. The previous record had been a little over 150,000 people reading. Each day we saw the new tally growing by tens of thousands. On the official date, at exactly noon we gathered the entire school in the gym to read together. The LCD projector showed us the Web site's tally of over 560,000 people reading in all 50 states and in at least 27 different countries. In subsequent days our social studies lessons in fourth and fifth grades featured map reading and geography activities where students calculated distances and the times when readings occurred in different time zones. In addition, we issued a challenge to students to read as many books as possible in the week remaining before we attended the film. Pupils in all grades were asked to estimate the total number of books the student body would read during that period. The student in each grade whose estimate was closest to the total would win a prize. Throughout the week students in each class kept tallies of how many books they read. These tallies were collected by volunteers from fourth grade, who also created a giant poster of a bar graph that we hung in the main lobby. Each day we updated our graph so that all students could see the progress of our reading challenge. By the end of that week our 271 students had read more than 600 books.

Our schoolwide study of the novel, and the subsequent field trip allowed teachers the opportunity to develop many cross-curricular lessons. Artistic bulletin boards and other related art projects, language arts, character education, and social studies were all evident during this project. The many math-related activities were an exciting way for our students to see mathematics skills integrated into a wide range of curricular areas. This project confirmed our strong belief in the importance of teaching math in an integrated manner. With a little creativity teachers can make math come alive for students in so many different ways. Our goal is to make our students see learning as a lifelong activity in which they joyfully participate. We welcome any and all new ideas that will help us make math education fun and exciting for our students.

Sincerely,

John C. Anzul

Principal

John's voice is a clear affirmation that teaching and learning mathematics in unexpected places and times throughout the day is not only possible, but essential. We have an obligation to our students, their parents, and our sense of humanity to help students to think in critically important ways about themselves and their world.

TEACHER AS RESEARCHER THOUGHTS

1. Observe your students at recess. What choices do they make? Who plays together and who doesn't? Do girls play with boys or is recess play mostly a gender-segregated activity? What might be done to help students broaden their social contacts?

2. What characterizes the interactions between your community and school?

3. How can individual grades work toward a shared math focus?

4. How might individual content areas work toward a math-integrated concentration?

Chapter 8

What Do Parents Know?

Math in the Garden: One Parent's Pondering

Math, love, and gardening are not words that fit together easily in the same sentence for most of us, if in fact we think about loving, math, and gardening at all, let alone together. Most of us see a garden and measure it not in feet and inches, volumes of soil, or amounts of water needed. Our measure is of its beauty or how well it's kept up. A garden, whether shaped by man or nature, conjures up some clear images in our minds about what a garden is and where it is to be found. Gardens are to be found in the real world or in books. The same can be said about love. It, too, can be found in both the real world or in books. Now math, or MATHEMATICS, for most of us, is to be found only in books. Nature and math are opposites, like day and night.

Looking up the word "math," you might find a definition like this: Mathematics—the science of numbers and their operations, interrelations, combinations, generalizations, and abstractions, and of space configurations and their structures, measurement, transformations, and generalizations.

Even after reading the definition of math—what is it? And how does it differ from arithmetic, or computation? It makes my mind spin. This number thing does not come easy for me. But even so, I know in my heart of hearts that every time I step into my garden, I am surrounded by both growing things and math. How do I know? Simple. I look at the wooden boxes I have measured, cut, and nailed to make my flowerbeds. I look closely at the veins in the leaves; the way they branch off from each other with mathematical precision, the symmetry and asymmetry, the patterns and fractals, images throughout, in my garden. Through these means nature tells me—if numbers do not control, can they help to explain the beauty of the growing things about me?

Whether math is the glue, the instruction manual, or the language to explain everything is not as important to me as the fact that numbers play a part in nature. Flowers, for example, can be described as colors, structure, chemistry, and numbers. Most of the books that discuss math in nature are beyond my understanding, but just because something is hard for me to understand does not make it any less beautiful to see.

Looking up the word "garden," you might find a definition like this: Garden—a plot of ground where herbs, fruits, flowers, or vegetables are cultivated. To this definition of garden I would add "a great place to see numbers at play."

This piece was written by André, one of the parents in the *In Addition* afterschool program. In our work with the children and parents in this program, we strived to bring math to life so that they might begin to see math everywhere, and in turn, make doing math and solving math problems more relevant. During one of our parent meetings we asked that each person take a few minutes and write about where they find math in their lives—to see their worlds through a mathematical lens and to put their thoughts down on paper. As parents shared their thoughts it was an eye-opener for many to see the variety of ways people experienced math. One mother shared that she struggles with math while trying to estimate the cost of gas and mileage when planning family travel to Grandma's house; a father reported that he uses math to figure the areas of rooms in his carpet installation work; a mother wrote about the intricacies of family budgeting. André talked to the group about the time in his garden as his private space in which to think and to "get away from it all." Seeing math as everywhere in one's life is essential to overcoming math anxiety and any feelings of dread that are commonly associated with the discipline. Such a math awareness also helps us to respond to children when they ask, "When am I ever going to use this?"

WHAT *DO* PARENTS KNOW?

We interviewed more than 100 parents of third, fourth, and fifth graders in the course of the last 4 years in connection with the *In Addition* afterschool program. While the interviews focused generally on how they view and use math, they are free flowing and ask each parent interviewee to set most of the direction. Much of what parents shared during these talks fell into three themes:

1. I still have a lot of math anxiety. Parents talked about "being afraid of math," and "having a lot of difficulties." The following four statements are examples of the many responses shared by the parents describing their own lingering math anxieties:

   "I want to help my child even if it means facing my own math fears."

"My father was brilliant in math—and I've always felt challenged by it. My teachers were never really welcoming to me to help me understand. In high school I had a lot of trouble. I went to a very hard math teacher there, and he tutored me outside of class. On the one hand he tutored me—but in class he ridiculed me. It was always a negative experience and I am still hesitant about math."

"I have a 4-year-old and I have a feeling that when I get to her I'm going to be scared again. It's not going to be easier."

"I was afraid of math. I still find it frightening helping my child with her homework."

"An instance where I looked at her homework and I said wow this is really too hard for me I can't do this and she said, 'No I can do it Daddy. I can do it and she showed me how to do it.' So I thought that was pretty cool."

2. I want my child to have better experiences with math than I did.

"I don't want my child to repeat my math history."

"I can always recall having a lot of difficulties with math and no one seeming to care because I was a girl. I avoided all difficult math classes because they thought I would be a secretary or work in home economics. They really steered us in the direction they wanted us to go. If you balance your checkbook that's all you needed. It's different now."

"When I saw my daughter was having trouble with math I immediately thought to myself that I don't want her to be like me. I didn't ever overcome my math phobia."

"I know how difficult it was for me—always look for things that are interesting for my kids. I don't want them to have the same experience."

A clear pattern of concern threads through most of the parent interviews; an undeniable desire expressed by parents that their children's mathematical learning be far less stressful than their own. Parents reported that it is often this distress and apprehension connected with past math learning that prevents them from communicating with the school and teachers. They fear to appear stupid, pushy, or less than intelligent. Further:

"Many parents feel they are not looked at as a person of worth. And so I guess when you become a parent you have to decide— 'It's not about me anymore. It's about the extension of me, my child.'"

Such sacrifices need not be made. Parents must not feel depersonalized or conclude that school is not about them. In the best sense, schools must embrace students, their parents, and the broader community.

3. My child deserves to be treated like an individual in school.

"I want school to give my child your attention; be mindful of my child's needs."

"I feel somehow, if teachers could move into the individual child. I know they don't have much time in the day, but there are lots of days in the year. If you could take each child individually—to get to know that child—to take 5 minutes every day in groups and work to and talk to get to know him and to make that child feel he is an important piece of the puzzle. Maybe then he could perform."

"Even if you spoil the kids rotten. It is essential to make them feel it is safe at school. This is a sanctuary."

"The school belongs to the children. Give them their moment to shine."

The parents with whom we talked did not deny that they wanted their children to pass tests. Such a denial would have been illogical. Their discussion around the issue did, however, clarify their desire for a particular educational environment that embraced test taking and so much more.

The three themes made a clear statement that parents, to a person, never lost sight of the fact that their children were persons—with talents, feelings, and needs. How their children were treated in school was given paramount importance—long before parents discussed tests. This is a perfectly reasonable and long-accepted educational stance. It almost goes without saying. However, in these days of pressures on schools "to produce" and to see that production in terms of test scores, the voices of these parents serve as wise reminders and counterbalances. When children feel respected, powerful, and productive this is directly related to how they are seen at home and at school and how they are asked to learn. Teachers who understand this and who consistently strive to actualize it are essential.

THERE SHOULD BE MORE TO SCHOOL THAN PASSING TESTS

It is a commonly held assumption that parents' concerns about math education are driven by "making sure their child passes the test." Though this may be true, it is much too simplistic an accounting of parents' concerns. What we learned in our interviews is a deeper, more complex, motivating explanation. Parents expressed their own math histories as more often than not challenging, fearful, and frightening. No parents want their child to be challenged to the point of frustration and failure or to be frightened and fearful in any circumstance. These are parents whose self-esteem, relative to their mathematics ability, is quite low.

The myth that parents cannot understand teaching and learning in a variety of modes—or are not interested in doing so—should have been laid to rest ages ago. I fear it is still alive. This seems particularly so when parents are poor, do not appear fluent in English, or have a variety of other cultural experiences different from "what is expected" in particular classrooms and schools. What follows is a story that concerns recent immigrant parents.

I was asked by a principal of an elementary school in Brooklyn to work with a group of Russian immigrant parents about how they might reinforce mathematics learning in the home. The first of my visits was to focus on the importance of providing their children with opportunities to think and to ask questions. An interpreter was present because only a handful of parents spoke any English. The workshop began with my asking them for their definition of mathematics. A few parents responded with "numbers," "adding and dividing," and "manipulating figures to do problems." Most parents were silent so I went on to explain why mathematics was more than the arithmetic of adding, subtracting, multiplying, and dividing. Mathematics was also about interpreting information and making sense of numbers to understand budgets, weight loss, recipes, and miles traveled. I mentioned a variety of jobs that require mathematics such as architecture, carpet laying, engineering, shop keeping, ice cream selling, tailoring, and manufacturing.

I provided the following example as one alternate way of engaging children in mathematics. It is true that children can become proficient at multiplying 297 times 13 by memorizing a procedure and facts. But by asking your child to plan a meal that will cost under $7.00 to prepare, you are requiring a complex and real process that rests on more than procedural knowledge to figure out the answer. Children deserve to know what real mathematics is and have opportunities to solve interesting problems that they care about.

If we want learning to be lasting then we need to encourage real-life problem solving and the asking of questions.

After describing several more examples of ways to foster thinking with their children, one father asked to speak: "But we are hurting our children in this American system to teach them to think. The test is multiple-choice, so you must be quick to answer. If our children THINK, they will not get a good grade. This is a problem because we need our children to get good grades in this America."

I silently agreed with him and responded that I understood his dilemma. However, I also said, "But we must believe that THINKING is always better than responding procedurally. Teaching our children to think about mathematics in real-world contexts, to look for reasonableness in their thinking, and to be curious about what they find out will always serve them well. This will not detract from what they need to know to pass tests in the American system." There were some nods of agreement. Next I put the following on the blackboard.

$$
\begin{array}{r}
409 \\
+306 \\
\hline
85
\end{array}
$$

I asked the parents if this solution was reasonable. Many said, "No" and when I asked why, they agreed that the answer cannot be 85 because we are adding "more than 400 and more than 300."

"Would your children think the same way?"

"Yes, of course."

"And what does this mean about children and math?"

Here there was excited group talk—in English and Russian—and one mother spoke at its end, "You are saying that our children can think in this way—can reason—and that this will help them do better in math."

Enough said.

WHO SAID PARENTS DON'T CARE?

To think that parents don't care is, in one sense, an educational cop-out and, in another, a biased elitist vision. It is the stance of this book that all parents care about their children and want them to succeed in school and society. But many parents do not get involved for a variety of reasons—often their experiences in growing up were different from those in which they now find themselves or they are overcome with work and attempts to keep the family together. Sometimes they feel inadequate. This was described by the parents in the preceding section.

We have experienced some parent stories that exemplify their caring. Jeff is a single father whose wife is in prison. He is raising two sons, one in second grade and the other in fourth grade. Jeff attended the *In Addition* parent meetings every month even though he had to leave work early in order to get to our meetings on time. This was not something he did on a whim. When we questioned parents about how the parent meetings served them, Jeff said, "These meetings make me feel like I am being a good parent. I'm always thinking I am not doing right by my boys. But when I come here I leave thinking I did something for them that will mean something for their future."

John attended our meetings and was the most enthusiastic participant. He was always accompanied by his daughter, one of the *In Addition* fifth graders. We assumed John brought her because he didn't have anyone to take care of her during those hours. It was not until our spring retreat that we found the real reason. John can't read. We learned this when he and his family arrived at the retreat without blankets or sleeping bags. We had written on the permission form that everyone needed to bring warm bedding—either blankets or sleeping bags—because the cabins were not heated and the temperature might drop to near freezing. Upon realizing John's family was without any blankets, we immediately found them some appropriate bedding. At this point John told us that he didn't know how to read and that this embarrassed him mightily. He limited his attendance at school functions to those where he could bring his daughter because he was self-conscious and ill-at-ease. His desire to attend the *In Addition* meetings and retreats, knowing his secret might be discovered, is a testimony to how much he cared about the education of his children. He wanted more for his children than he himself left school with. Before the weekend's conclusion we talked with John about helping him learn how to read and arranged meetings with him so we could start.

Oliver is thoughtful, soft-spoken, and articulate. He shared that he and his wife had children at a very young age. He has worked hard to support his family and came on the weekend retreat to support his son. Oliver himself did not attend college. On this occasion he was part of a parent group seated in a circle in the dining hall while the children were off on a math measurement hike. The discussion was about what parents wanted for their children from the schools. Most people said that it was important that the schools prepare their children to do well so that they might get into college. They wished that they had had an opportunity to go to college and that it was their most fervent desire for their children to do so. Quietly, Oliver began to speak. He disagreed. He wanted MORE for his sons. He wanted them to love learning, to enjoy what they do, and to always feel comfortable and accepted. He knows that learning is more than passing a test. His opinion is that schools are about labeling children and that most of the labels are harmful. He is considering home schooling his young son when he reaches high school age because he believes the school system will not offer his son a rich environment for learning and growing; or will be a place that his son will look forward to attending for 7 hours a day, 5 days a week. Oliver is also not convinced that college will provide his child a better future than will high school.

These three parents are a few among millions who debunk the myth that some parents "just don't care about their children's education." Even faced with the toughest of circumstances, these parents appear to put their situations in perspective. They do this willingly in order to do whatever is necessary to ensure not only their children's school success but also their success and happiness in life.

MATH-IN-THE-WOODS: BRIDGING PARTNERSHIPS

During the retreat, on an early Saturday morning just after breakfast chores were completed, we gathered the parents together at one end of the dining hall to introduce the bridge-building activity. The children were engaged elsewhere in a morning kite-making activity.

The instructions to parents were:

> In groups of five or six each, your challenge is to build a bridge. The constructed bridge must be 3 feet high and span a minimum of 6 feet. Your bridge must also be sturdy enough to hold each member walking across it. You may only use this rope and any materials you find in the woods or in the vicinity of where you decide to build your bridge. You have a little more than an hour to complete your task.

The *In Addition* team had assigned parents to the groups beforehand. Spouses were separated to work on different teams. Parents huddled in their newly formed groups and after a short while all but one group had wandered off toward the wooded area in search of materials.

The only clue we had about their work in progress stemmed from one remaining group that clung close to the campsite, in clear view—talking and laughing. Soon they could be seen dragging such items as a trash can, a boulder that was half the size of a plastic lawn chair, and several cement blocks found under the porch of cabin 12. They brought the items into the center of the large common lawn area.

At the end of the hour all groups came together in the cafeteria. The energy in the room was palpable—dialogue and posturing across group and squeals of laughter made it difficult to get everyone's attention. By this time the children had returned from their kite-making project and were animatedly questioning the parents about what they had done.

After some brief discussions we trouped out together, all 64 of us and proceeded to visit each of the five bridge constructions. At every stop parents took center stage in sharing with the group how they went about making their bridge, naming the bridges, and proudly demonstrating the bridges' strength by parading each group member across to the cheers and applause of the viewing crowd.

This activity became key to how many of these parents now understand *In Addition*. After talking about what happened, how they worked together and what they learned, they made a link to the value of real-life math experiences. Previously they had known that their children enjoyed *In Addition* and seemed to learn math while so engaged. But it was with the bridge-building project that they broke through to a deeper understanding about how learning might and could happen.

SUGGESTIONS FOR BRIDGING PARENT HELP

Studies show most parents and teachers want children to succeed in school and throughout their lives. Children get a sense that education is valued if parents are involved in some way in the school community. Joyce Epstein of Johns

Hopkins University (2006) developed a framework for identifying different kinds of parent involvement that seem particularly pertinent to the topics at hand in this book. Epstein's work is based on the assumption that bridging partnerships between home and school will help to attain the goal of shaping meaningful learning in school and beyond for children. Her framework lists six types of parent involvement:

1. Parenting—helping families understand learning opportunities at home.
2. Communicating—maintaining open communication between home and school and between school and home.
3. Volunteering—actively recruiting parents' assistance.
4. Learning at home—how to help at home.
5. Decision making—enlisting parents in joining school decision-making committees and events.
6. Collaborating with the community—using community resources to strengthen learning.

Though most parents are willing to get involved, they often don't know how to find their way into the school culture, especially if they themselves are new to the community and school. Many parents are not sure how to help with their children's learning at home for fear of doing it "wrong" and creating more problems than assistance. This creates a situation of isolation and estrangement between home and school for many because they do not share common schooling experiences or racial and ethnic backgrounds. This makes it necessary that teachers be more "multi-conscious" in order to be sensitive to different identities. The bottom line is that "having educators understand the experiences of their students and the families from which they come will make them better, more effective teachers" (Edwards, 2005).

The following letter is written by Jae Goodwin. Jae is not only a good friend, but also an exceptional teacher whose teaching ideas are woven throughout this book. She is writing to parents because she passionately believes that if we strive to actively include parents in the learning process, their children, our students, benefit tenfold. Her plea adds an "authentic voice" to the ideas put forth in this chapter.

Jae's letter exemplifies that humility is a way to build bridges by showing parents that teachers don't always know everything. She also wanted to help parents understand that tests do not always tell us all that students can do and that understanding is achieved through "doing." Jae also provides further support for the beliefs highlighted in chapter 3: teaching requires more listening than telling, and reality-based learning helps students to understand.

Dear Parents,

When your child comes home eager to teach you lattice multiplication and your pencil is poised and your lips are just about to utter, "Here let me show you a quicker way ... 8 times 2 is 16, put down the 6 and carry the 1," RESIST the temptation. After all what does carry the 1 mean? In actuality there is no 1, it is a 10! I do not want my students carrying any 1s, I want them to understand what they are doing, what it means. Contrary to the rote way many of us learned, my students are learning number sense; they are making meaning of math.

My classroom is a hive of activity. Students are "doing" math the way you and I do it but never talk about it. Most of us are not doing long division in the grocery store; we are estimating our groceries along the way. We do not take out a calculator to figure out what the dress would cost with a sale price of 15%, we take 10%, cut it in half, add together and subtract. Hours spent in the classroom measuring with a ruler will not help you in Home Depot unless you have that ruler in your pocket. My students can estimate with personal measurements like their fingernail, which they have discovered, is roughly one centimeter. These kids really *know* what a centimeter is.

In graduate school, I was required to take a class on teaching elementary math. The professor put us in groups and asked us if we could make various sized shapes with different pattern block pieces. My colleagues were effortlessly creating them and running to the chart paper with their answers. As I sat there, I began to feel the same feeling of dread I had in high school geometry washing over me. No matter how hard I tried I just didn't see what they saw. When the professor kindly came over with a bucket of pattern blocks, and showed me how I could move and flip the pieces it was as if the ubiquitous light bulb had popped on. I have never forgotten that and when I see my own students with that look on their faces I give them manipulatives to use. I put things in their hands and let them explore and make meaning for themselves. I know that that is the way they will understand. You, too, can do this at home with your children. Offer things like handfuls of macaroni that kids can divide into piles to understand division. Let them help you cook so they can see what two-thirds of a cup is. Resist the temptation to "show" them calculations that they may pick up quickly but will not lead to meaning.

There is so much pressure on teachers and students to perform well on standardized tests. I don't think the answer lies in more calculation. Every day my students show me that the calculation comes once the understanding is achieved. After my students completed the mathematics testing this year, I asked them what was easy for them and what was hard. Over and over they said, "The things we *did* were really easy to remember but the things we just read about or were supposed to memorize were really hard."

Respectfully,
Jae Goodwin

HELPING PARENTS FEEL VALUED

The book titled *Seven Blind Mice* (Young, 1992) is a story about seven mice, each of a different color, who one by one set out to identify the strange "thing" in their midst. As six mice study the "thing" briefly and each quickly makes a variety of claims—"It is a snake," "It is a fan"—the seventh, and last mouse, examines the "thing" lengthily, up and down and across and comes back to claim that the "thing" is an elephant. The moral of the story is that knowing parts rarely brings clarity. Understanding comes from knowing more of the whole. This phenomenon is known as synergy. "Synergy or synergism (from the Greek *synergos*, συνεργός meaning working together) refers to the phenomenon in which two or more discrete influences or agents acting together create an effect greater than that predicted by knowing only the separate effects of the individual agents. It is originally a scientific term. Often (but not always ... the prediction is the sum of the effects each is able to create independently" (www. wikipedia.com, 2007).

When considering the children we teach, it takes knowing as many pieces as possible about each child to reach a tentative understanding. In this, learning from parents is crucial. Parents must know that their perspective on the child is critical if we are to find ways to help each child to learn and to develop in unique ways (Spielberg. 2006). Parents most often have much to contribute to how teachers understand each child—what they enjoy doing, what is happening at home that may influence how they are interacting in the classroom, the activities that cause anxiety as well as those that bring joyful anticipation. Parents often are aware of child interactions that might have an impact on their children.

As reported in the December 7, 2006, issue of *New York Teacher*, Hillary Rodham Clinton addressed the ninth annual Parent Conference of 3,600 cheering parents. They stood and applauded because Senator Clinton had just spoken these words: "Thank you for caring about your children. Thank you for being our partners—because our city's teachers cannot do this work alone."

DIFFERENT AND EQUAL

This next piece highlights the importance and need for a multicultural perspective on teaching and learning that meets the needs of the culturally diverse populations we encounter in our classrooms today. It is the responsibility of teachers and administrators to recognize the serious disconnect experienced by many African American, Hispanic, and other minority children in urban public schools. We often become insensitive to their educational needs and find ourselves blaming these children for their own academic failures (Cobb, 2002;

Kozol, 2000). It is within the realm of the classroom or school for parents and teachers to influence a great deal the factors that contribute to this phenomenon and to empower minority children and their families. First, we must recognize the contributions of ethnic groups and celebrate the rich cultural heritage of *all* students. The silence of minority families may be a result of our inability to respond to their "social, economic, emotional, and, especially their educational needs, and our misgivings regarding their place in public schools and their potential contributions to our society" (Trueba, 1989, p. 109).

Betsy, a dear friend and colleague who also teaches from a problem-posing perspective and who views critical analysis as a part of our everyday lives, tells her own story about an experience involving her son. In Betsy's words, her story exemplifies "why our children and our citizens need to have more support in developing deep, critical thinking and transformative action. Daily, I see needs for all of us as citizens to use the skills and generative forms of knowledge promoted in this book."

Betsy moved from El Paso, Texas, with her three sons to a small city in the Midwest. She wanted to locate a school in which Spanish was taught at the middle-school level, as that was the language of her children's father and she wanted that part of their heritage to be maintained. Although she was uncomfortable with the lack of children of color, lack of students from working-class families, and lack of children from single-parent families in a private school she found, she enrolled her sons because she could not find another school where Spanish was being taught.

Betsy tells of a time when she was "invited" by the teachers into the school conference room and asked if she was able to spend much time with her three boys. The teachers and administrator patronizingly acknowledged that they were aware of her busy schedule as a single parent. She explained to the teachers and the administrator that during many years as a single parent she and her sons shared many valuable moments, routines, and family customs that helped to establish very strong relationships among each other.

They nodded and went on to report to Betsy about her son's apparent disrespect of two teachers in two different classes and his inappropriate behavior. Betsy assured them disrespect was not tolerated in her family. When she queried the teachers about the disrespect and inappropriate behavior, Betsy was told that her son had a habit of not looking at the teacher when being spoken to and often looking down or not answering when being reprimanded. The teachers in this school were not aware that in some cultures it is considered impolite for a child to look an adult in the face.

Betsy goes on to share another disturbing incident. She received a call at her office from the dean of the middle school who told her she was suspending her son from school for 2 days and from the bus for 2 weeks because of an incident on the bus.

When Betsy asked what the incident was, she also asked the dean if she had talked with her son or other students on the bus to hear their side of the story. The dean said she had not, at which time Betsy demanded a meeting with all parties involved, including her son, before any actions were to be taken. On her way to the arranged meeting Betsy was met by four of her son's friends who also rode the same bus. They said, "It wasn't him; it was all of us. And we were just goofing on each other—nobody said anything to the bus driver." At the meeting the dean explained what the bus driver had said and then asked Betsy's son his side of the story.

The dean acknowledged that there were very big differences in the two versions, but that since the bus driver had filed a formal complaint according to her impressions, disciplinary action must be taken. When Betsy asked how the bus driver had singled out her son the dean replied, "Well, she didn't know his name, but knew it was a funny, different name. Then we showed her school pictures of all the kids on that bus." A lineup. "And she picked out your son right away."

It became apparent as the meeting progressed that the bus driver had singled out Betsy's son because he did not look like the rest of the kids from Minnesota with his black curly hair and dark skin. The only training the bus driver had received for her job was a video on gangs in which all the "bad" boys were either Latino or African American.

When Betsy asked if this was fair, the dean shifted in her seat and responded directly to Betsy's son, "If one is not white or middle class, one must work harder, dress better, make better grades, and make more money to be equal." When Betsy showed her outrage at this statement the dean responded with "I know, it's not right. But that's just the way things are, and I don't think we can do anything to change it."

This story points out the necessity to be mindful of cultural differences in our classrooms. If any people have any hopes of affecting change, isn't it those of us who work in education? All students deserve the right to be equal members of the school community and differences perceived as "different, but equal."

Parents are a valuable resource for teachers and schools. They provide insight into each child's individual strengths and weaknesses, as well as being the important link between home, school, and community. Being validated for one's contribution is the stuff that keeps all of us going—validation can come in the form of a public announcement such as the one spoken by Senator Clinton, or often from even more powerful sources, teachers, and school administrators.

Such a sense of how our individuality plays out in distinctly different ways in our learning patterns is exemplified in an article written by one of the *In Addition* parents. In the article below, Thierry, the parent of one of the fourth-grade participants, points out one of the essential elements of the *In Addition* program: learning must be shaped to individual learners.

DOES ONE SIZE FIT ALL?

The final piece I will share in this chapter is an essay written by Thierry, one of the *In Addition* parents. I have placed it last because I find his message one of great importance and probably the most difficult to carry out.

Everyone knows these "one size fits all" socks, size 9 to 11. Well they are not ideal for a man with shoe size 7 because the socks will often lump up in his shoes either at the toes, the heel, or both. But not many people are actually adversely affected since the great majority of American men have shoe sizes between 9 and 11. Also these kind of socks can be mass produced in great countries like China and India and sold cheaply in the street, or for a lot more in upscale stores. That "one size fits all" reminds me of my grand-aunt Paulette who was writing for a woman's magazine. Every month she gave new parents great advice on how their children must be raised. Aunt Paulette explained to them, for example, that when a child is having a tantrum one must stay cool, explain to the child that she must be reasonable, give her a time out, never raise a hand on her, and so on. She must have been pretty good at it since she contributed to this column for quite a few years. In the meantime her only son Michel, my mom's cousin, was the most misbehaved child ever in our family, had to be bailed out of jail at 16 after driving without a license, dropped out of school a year later, got somehow stuck 2 years with the army in Korea before returning home to become successively a disco club manager, restaurant owner, small-time real estate developer, and more recently, an art investor who swindled old ladies. Michel is so much fun; just don't do any business with him. Aunt Paulette must have learned so much with him to be able to give great "one size fits all" pieces of advice!

Like her I thought I knew it all when a few years back my daughter Carly was 3, and our son Ralph was about to be born. Carly's first three years had been tough for the well-educated professional I was. I believed I learned a lot, and I imagined I could apply it straight out of the box to our new son. I realized that girls and boys are different but felt only a few adjustments would be required. In fact, I found out very quickly the children were so different, and not only because of different sex. Carly is a pretty quiet child, with a good sense of humor, who likes to play by herself setting up complex "pretend" scenario games. Ralph can't be shut up, takes everything to heart, and needs someone else to take part in his many physical activities and games. One of them is a bit like me: will "learn fast after being explained to for a while," but will persevere until the job gets done. The other one will catch on to things extremely quickly, but will also become frustrated if something doesn't work out right away. They are two very different individuals, reacting so differently that applying the "one size fits all" rule seems silly.

The "one size fits all" rule may sometimes be practical, however, or even necessary. Looking at a class of 30 kids I can imagine how challenging it would be for a teacher to customize his approach to each and every one. But the best ones do. Luckily we parents never have that many children and therefore can use a little less of the "one size fits all." The *In Addition* program seems concerned enough with the issue, and accepts the idea that one size doesn't necessarily fit all. They also made me write about it.

Finally, history shows the drawbacks, or even atrocities, resulting from past attempts to fit entire societies into one size or model. We all remember Adolf's Nazi Germany, Joe's and Mao's communist Soviet Union and China. They pushed that "one size fits all" rule to the limits.

TEACHER AS RESEARCHER THOUGHTS

1. What are the ways I reach out to parents?
2. What is the nature of talk about parents in the teacher's room?
3. What happens to children's engagement when parents are included in the classroom?
4. Create your own set of parent stories. Decide on a few open-ended questions and conduct several talk sessions with individual parents.
5. Invite parents to a "focus group" discussion about their math histories and the math learning of their children.

Chapter 9

Is Thinking about Thinking
Just a Play on Words?

I wrote in my autobiography that it frustrated me when teachers taught only to the kids who "got it." I found that my math teachers seemed to have fun with the advanced students and got frustrated with those of us who were not getting the concepts. My favorite thing about *this* course was that it did not feel like people who struggled more with math were left out or left behind. Instead it felt like we learned more when people asked questions about what they did not understand.

I think this atmosphere was created partly because the projects and homework we worked on had multiple entry points. They challenged all of us, but were also accessible to all of us, even though the group was made of some people who currently teach math and others who have been avoiding the subject for years. It seems like open-ended questions often allowed for this idea of multiple entry-points.

I never realized before this class how truly open you can leave a question. I am amazed that in a few short weeks I have totally left behind the idea that math is about learning a set of rules in order to answer a set of direct questions. When we saw the responses to the "Post Family Problem" I was really blown away. I love that some children made charts, some made graphs, and some wrote really creative responses. It wasn't the type of word problem I grew up on where you just had to add the correct word to the end of a number. Like "Janie was left with 3 apples." Instead, it allowed for kids of all mathematical abilities to challenge themselves and think creatively. Their responses definitely changed the way I think about math as both a learner and prospective teacher. Of course I also realize it must take a lot of work and practice to create an environment that would produce answers like the ones we saw. However, as with our own course, it has changed my

155

thinking just to see that it is *possible* to have a fun, creative and challenging math class.

The previous passage is the self-evaluation of a graduate student articulating what she learned as a result of her participation in a mathematics methods course. Self-assessment is the final assignment in the math methods course and is designed to help learners understand what they know and how they came to know it. The Post Family Problem that Ellen referenced in her self-evaluation is one I use with graduate students to help them to think about elements of a classroom community. The Post Family Problem is this:

Solve this problem.

Give as complete an answer as possible.

Explain your thinking.

    All-Day Tickets

    Adult $18

    Child $9

    Family $50

The Post family read this sign. Mr. Post said, "I think it would be cheaper for our family to buy individual adult and child tickets." His daughter, Maria, thought it would be cheaper for them to buy a family ticket. What do you think the Post family should do?

I ask students to solve the problem by themselves. After 10 minutes, I instruct the students to put away their answers to the problem as I show a collection of fifth-grade responses to the same Post Family Problem. Before I share the student solutions, I ask that the class consider the classroom from which I collected these responses—what is it like and how would they describe the teacher of this classroom?

Two of the fifth-grade solutions involved elaborate charts with columns showing different sizes of families and the costs for each of the different family configurations. One of the students explained how the graph was constructed and added, "If there is only Mr. Post and Maria in the Post family, then Mr. Post is right, but if there are more than two people in the Post family then Maria might be right. The most important thing is to know how many Posts there are but the problem doesn't tell the amount of people in the Post family, so we can't be sure."

Students wrote a variety of comments such as:

> "With three children and two adults the cheapest way to do it is to buy a family ticket, or just not to go."

"You must take into consideration that a child might be old enough to be an adult. You also don't know what family means. Does it mean mother, father, grandmother, grandfather, aunt, uncle, cousins?"

"To solve the problem I am gong to assume that there are three people in the Post Family: a daughter, a mother, and a child."

"The Post family has five people in it: a mom, her friend, and three children. Their names are Maria, Vicki, and Mark."

"Now, if there were more than three people in the Post family, a family ticket would be cheaper. What I don't get is what if there are 10 people or more in a family, would it still be $50 for a family ticket? Now that's cheap! What is the age group for children's tickets: ages 7 to 16? Do 6 years and under get in free or are they counted as an individual ticket?"

My favorite response is:

"With the information given Mr. Post is right, but you can't stop wondering what if there was one more child, or a child old enough so he or she has to buy an adult ticket? In that case the daughter is right. Or maybe if one of them works there maybe they could get a discount? What if there was only one parent with the child or children? Then it would be cheaper to buy separate tickets. These are many different ways this can be put but there are probably thousands and each with a different answer."

After sharing the fifth-grade solutions to this problem we engage in a lively class discussion about how these young students came to think like this, rather than giving a quick "not enough information" reply to the question posed. This discussion and the collaborative, as well as individual, reflection that accompanies the dialogue are significant for many graduate students and often create new insights and shifts in thinking about the teaching and learning of mathematics. The graduate students continue to reflect on this lesson throughout the semester, as many of them make mention of this in their final self-evaluations as a critical turning point in their learning journey.

In this chapter I first discuss reflection from many angles: what reflection is, critical reflection, and collaborative reflection. I will explain in depth my experiences and research with self-evaluation and briefly explore the wider implications of critical thinking for society and the need to model reflective thinking for our students. There is a growing need to attract more students to study in the field of mathematics. This issue will be examined in some depth, in addition to a look at the implications of critical thinking for other content areas. This chapter ends with an urban teacher's reflections and thoughts on his experiences as he worked with fourth-grade students on their reflective writing in math class.

WHAT IS REFLECTION?

There is general agreement that reflection is a deliberate process. The majority of definitions consider reflection as a process of thinking about experience with the intention to improve thinking and direct future behavior. Van De Walle (2006) explains the need for reflection in our mathematics classrooms: "constructing knowledge requires reflective thought, actively thinking about or mentally working on an idea. Reflective thought means sifting through existing ideas to find those that seem to be the most useful in giving meaning to the new idea" (p. 23). However, in schools there is often precious little time allotted for reflection, for teachers or students to think about their thinking with such careful, thoughtful deliberation. Donald Schön (1983), a leading theorist in the area of reflective practice, suggested a process that allows for learning to occur from a careful examination of practice. Schön (1991) also explored different professions in order to understand how practitioners in various fields go about solving problems in the action of "doing" their profession. He found many professionals know more than they can articulate about their practice and actions. In order to meet the challenges of their professions, practitioners rely on spontaneous behaviors learned in the course of their work. Schön reported that professionals frame and reframe complex and ambiguous problems by evaluating and testing out what they think is going on and modifying their practice as a result of this reflection. This is what he refers to as "reflection in action."

Critical Reflection

Jack Mezirow, also known for his work on transformative dimensions of learning, made a clear distinction between reflection and critical reflection. Reflection is "a generic term for those intellectual and affective activities in which individuals engage to explore their experiences in order to lead to new understandings and appreciation" (1990, p. 167). Mezirow states that reflection is an assessment of how and why we have perceived, thought, felt, or acted. He defines critical reflection as the process of challenging established and habitual patterns that govern how we make sense of our world, others, and ourselves. Mezirow believes critical reflection is transformative because it enables us to alter our beliefs and to correct the way we solve problems; it is the process of correcting errors in reasoning and attitudes. According to Mezirow, to be critically reflective is to challenge the established definition of a problem being posed, examine assumptions, or perhaps find a new perspective or orientation from which to think about the dilemma and then posing it in a different way. The opening passage is an example of critical reflection. By her own admission, the Post Family responses created a dilemma for Ellen. She had previously believed that merely learning a set of rules or memorizing an algorithm would lead to successful problem solving. Once Ellen observed an approach to learning and solving problems that involved collaboration, imagination, and understanding, she critically reflected on what this meant for her as a classroom teacher. Her reasoning shifted. Ellen's teaching and learning framework now includes a more expansive perspective on what it means to be a problem solver and to teach children to solve problems.

Collaborative Reflection

Collaborative inquiry is a humanistic group activity to build new knowledge. By working, questioning, and reflecting on the ideas of one another, we are engaged in meaningful solving of dilemmas, questions, and problems and also extensions of knowledge and interpretations. In working collaboratively, we are more apt to avoid a manipulative, authoritarian-driven approach to knowledge construction. Discussions of the value of collaborative inquiry can be found in the writings of Dewey (1933/1998) and Vygotsky (1962/1969), as well as in more recent writings endorsing reflective thinking as essential to mathematical understanding (Carpenter, Franke, & Levi, 2003; Fosnot, 1996; Lambert, 1990; Yackel & Cobb, 1996). We assist our students to better understand the mathematics we teach by engaging them collaboratively in the learning process as self-directed learners. As children engage in collaborative inquiry projects they have a greater sense of control over the learning process as they experience pluralistic thinking and multiple strategies and solutions, collectively constructed (Resnick, 1987). Such cooperative building of ideas helps children learn how other people understand and make sense of ideas.

THE REFLECTIVE LEARNER

Self-evaluation is a research-based approach that has been found effective for individuals and groups to assess their learning by building a relationship to the learning process in unique ways (McVarish & Solloway, 2002). First, a learner must recognize her critical role in the assessment/evaluation of her learning. Second, the learner *must* reflect on what learning is and what constitutes evidence of learning and engaging in higher order thinking skills.

Throughout the semester teachers-to-be in the mathematics methods course assume conscious and explicit ownership and accountability for the choices and decisions they make concerning their learning in the course. Students are given some of the responsibility of deciding what is it they need to know and do in order to advance their thinking in the topics being taught. The expectation is for them to continuously reflect on how their reasoning and ways of thinking about teaching and learning are changing, shifting, or strengthening as the semester unfolds. They do this by keeping a reflective journal in which they write their thoughts, questions, and observations about mathematics teaching and learning. Students also reflect on the class activities each week on a 3-by-5 index card on which I write a response to and return to them the following week. At the end of the course students are asked to provide evidence that supports their assertions about what they have learned. They must document in their self-assessments the sources of learning evidence they claim. For example, Ellen did not merely claim to know that it is important to teach with open-ended questions. She clearly understood that her new understanding of the importance of providing challenging mathematics for children of all mathematical abilities stemmed from the Post Family Problem and accompanying classroom discussion. Seeing and talking about the Post family responses definitely changed her thinking about what it means to do mathematics. Ellen also was aware of why and when she had shifted her thinking about *all* students being capable of solving problems.

As students become stewards of their own learning the classroom shifts from an authoritarian, teacher-driven power structure to a community of learning in which the teacher is a participant offering another critical voice/perspective for the community of individuals to consider. The teacher's role is to provide a pedagogy that meets individual learning needs, course requirements, and the collective learning of the community. The leadership role, however, is that of a facilitator and supporter in balance with more traditional leadership roles. The goal is for all participants to work toward critical conversations in a process of inquiry. This helps ensure that all learners have opportunities to communicate ideas that are contemplated, tested, and argued so that individual and community teaching and learning frameworks can be developed.

Self-evaluation involves the learner in constructing an assessment of learning by reflecting on the new ideas that are developing in their teaching and learning schemas and being vigilant about finding evidence to support that she understands these new ideas and concepts and has incorporated them into her practice. Self-evaluation provides a framework for integrating rational thought and emotion in understanding cognition in the assessment process.

To further illuminate the experience of self-assessment, and in particular, the learner's perspective, I have included a poem, "the more or less of self assessment." This poem is a composite of 22 students' writings woven into a whole that describes self-assessment from the student perspective.

the more or less of self assessment   hmm

the idea of assessing my own learning, by its very virtue, created

more responsibility, more involvement, more connections
  to my own bucket of experiences, more reflection,
  more pushing myself harder to learn more …

whew

resulting in

being more focused on my learning, making more
  discoveries, becoming more personally responsible,
  and ending up with a more accurate grade.

more asking of "why"; more motivated to makes sense of things …

less reliance on teacher

more in control …

less being controlled …

therefore …

more accountable to myself

more listening … more aware of the world around me, more
  confidence now … perhaps the reason there is less resentment?

more community,

less competition

more relevant and meaningful, working
  more harder because it is my own.

more about learning, more about being my own
  thoughtful critic, less about a grade

more difficult being objective, wow, even more weird
  and uncomfortable doing this about me,

but …

I have been more myself because of it.

    These "bits" of insight from students who have spent an entire semester taking charge of their learning in ways they never experienced are inspirational. They leave little ambiguity about the power of self-assessing one's learning. These students declare a sense of ownership of the learning where there is less reliance on the teacher as authority. The goal of the learning was no longer a grade, but rather a more relevant, meaningful learning experience.

MOVING FROM THE COLLEGE CLASSROOM TO SELF-ASSESSMENT IN THE ELEMENTARY SCHOOL

It is critical for all of us in education to think about and reflect on "what is learning" and "what is evidence of learning" as an ongoing inquiry throughout our teaching careers. Every day as elementary school teachers we make important decisions based on our belief of what we consider learning and evidence of learning. As a teacher of teachers and pre-service teachers for over 15 years, and prior to that a teacher of elementary school children, it is my belief that something wonderful happens when learners of any age are charged with the responsibility for assessing their own learning when they are put in the driver's seat of mapping the learning journey route, for noting the landmarks as they travel, and for assessing the trip after reaching the destination.

The notion of constructing one's own learning and discovering and making meaning through connections to one's own uniquely individual experiences, both past and present, has been endorsed by progressive educators for decades (Brooks & Brooks, 1999; Dewey, 1929/1960, 1938/1963; Perkins, 1992). Therefore, it seems reasonable to assume that if the learner benefits from constructing the understanding, why wouldn't assessment of that learning experience reward the learner as well? If we are searching instead for active student involvement, the kind that necessitates relational understandings and connected learning in which personal and collaborative experience are valued more than authoritarian pronouncements, then the learner is in the best position to explain those relational understandings and connections. Reflecting on the learning episode and articulating what is known and what is the evidence to support one's knowing is not only a learner's responsibility, but also a learner's entitlement (McVarish & Solloway, 2002).

Teachers cannot assume that all learners have the same set of experiences or goals on which they place their learning. They need to become aware of the existence of alternate cultural norms that place value on specific forms of learning. Therefore, how can we judge each student with the same set of understandings/expectations or put them on a plane or continuum that sorts their learning into piles of yes/no, gets it/doesn't get it, understands/does not understand? What if we held students accountable for an explanation of what it is they know and understand and how they know that they understand it?

Think about what might happen to student engagement and learning if you explained to the class before a unit of study that each student would be responsible for telling you what he or she learned, if anything, at the end of the unit. Throughout the unit students keep journals, talk and work with others, and participate in classroom discussions. Make it clear to the students that at the end of the unit there will be no test. They will be responsible for telling you what they have learned, if anything, and how they came to learn this. I have done this many times with third-, fourth-, and fifth-grade students and it is quite remarkable what happens during the learning when students know ahead of time they will be asked to explain their learning at the conclusion of the unit of study.

BEING TRANSPARENT IN OUR THINKING PROCESSES

A goal of mine in this research work with self-assessment is to model a habit of reflection for teachers and learners that continuously asks what learning is and how we know when learning has taken place. Another focus is to develop a disposition for higher order thinking that includes nuanced judgment and interpretation, self-regulation of the thinking process, and a tolerance for ambiguity (Resnick, 1987).

Thinking about thinking brings me back to my own thoughts as an educator and the ways I think about how we as adults are responsible for helping young children to become critical in their thinking about themselves and the world in which they live. Providing our students with a multitude of opportunities to think, collaborate, and reflect is essential. It becomes equally necessary that we live out in our own lives mathematical thinking, and in general the critical thinking skills that we try to teach and model for our students. For example, educator colleagues and I have discussed at some length the implications of educational issues facing us in the 21st century. These informal exchanges of minds occur during lunches, faculty meetings, or casual gatherings late in the day, after classes. Our discussions include such topics as how to collect books to help a struggling new daycare facility that services immigrant racetrack workers, how we might develop a course of study to take students to New Orleans to do their student teaching, how to bring our students to the neighborhood senior care facility every month to play math games with groups of elderly men and women, and how to help students with their study of bullying. We share ideas, books, and concerns. We help each other grow and become better teachers and more caring citizens. It is not easy to find these collaborative reflection spaces in the everyday routines of an elementary school.

I taught at a school in Massachusetts where one teacher organized a monthly "gathering of the minds" group. She put flyers in everyone's mailbox—teachers, administrators, office help, and custodial staff. *"All I have to offer are cookies and my classroom. Come next Thursday at 3pm for an hour of talk without an agenda."* I went. Seven other teachers attended and one custodian poked his head in and asked for a cookie. The organizer of the group started with, "This is not a griping session. We are here to share any thoughts about our teaching, any new books we've read, or conferences we've attended. If you have an idea you've been thinking about and want to bounce it off the group, the floor is yours." The dialogue was what you might expect at that first meeting—talk of a new lesson that was tried and worked wonderfully, a novel method of classroom control someone had learned at a conference, and a suggestion for a whole school art fair. The meeting ended at 4 and another teacher volunteered her room 3 weeks later for the next meeting.

These meetings continued for the rest of the school year. They gradually became different in the kind of talk that was shared. The meetings were no longer about activities, but took on a deeper, more philosophical nature. Topics being discussed at the end of the year included a long discussion about Kozol's *Savage Inequalities* (1991) that lasted for several meeting times. We all left these meetings feeling a connection to teaching that was larger than our individual classrooms and community. Our sense of humanity was lifted to another level of awareness and concern.

As educators, we must be reflective critical thinkers if we expect our students to be the same. Would you promote the use of Colgate toothpaste if you use Tom's of Maine? The ultimate goal is that our students engage in reflective, critical, collaborative considerations, as we ourselves do. One way is to be transparent in our thinking to help our students experience the thought processes we use when we make decisions about teaching. Thinking about thinking is how we as educators continue to be learners. We need to be more explicit about the ways we do this. For example, "After reading your journal entries, I'm not sure if I planned that lesson in the best possible way for you to think more deeply about the concept of mixed fractions. I will have to think about what I might have done differently in order for you to make those real-life connections." "I've been thinking about what Tony said yesterday about why kids fight in our school. I agree with him that many fights are related to bullying, but I'm still thinking about the suggested solution to put bully monitors in the halls. I keep wondering if this might increase, rather than decrease, the episodes of bullying. Is the problem bullying or is it bigger than that—maybe the culture of the school? What do you think?"

When schools become communities of learning where members learn how to communicate with one another, who learn to work and solve problems collaboratively, and who feel a sense of ownership with the learning and the community, students have a model for what collaborative reflective behavior looks like. When teachers are themselves critical problem solvers who connect the mathematics they teach to the lives of their students, students are more apt to see mathematics as relevant, vital, and connected to their lives.

THE NEED FOR MORE MATHEMATICIANS

I worked very closely with Scott, a mathematician colleague, on ways to make my math education courses include the rigorous mathematics he felt was often missing from teacher education courses. In turn, I assisted him in using a more inquiry-based pedagogy in his mathematics courses. During this year-long collaboration our critical conversations often turned to the diminishing number of students who were seeking careers in mathematics. We spent hours discussing this issue. Our questions began to turn toward our role as educators and the ways in which we might help to alleviate this dilemma. How can we engage young learners in the work of mathematics in order to attract a more expansive and inclusive population of students wanting to further their education toward careers in mathematics? The need to foster in young learners the notion that their world is math-centered cannot be overemphasized. Every career or endeavor they will undertake has mathematics at its core. Architects, nurses, dancers, musicians, policemen, carpenters, journalists, computer technologists, interior designers, basketball players, and photographers are only a few of the career choices where mathematics is integral to the profession. Helping students to see the real-life math connections and work-related relevance is our obligation.

Scott and I began to research this problem. Since the late 1980s there has been a steady decline in the number of students studying mathematics in high school and college and an explosive increase in the number of jobs that require mathematical skills (NRC, 1989; NSB, 2004a; NSB, 2004b). This resulted in a national shortage of mathematics teachers and mathematicians as professionals and there is general agreement that this crisis will get even more severe in coming years. There has been research about students' images of mathematicians and the work that a mathematician does (Furinghetti, 1993; Livingstone & Izard, 1993; Picker & Berry, 2000; Rock & Shaw, 2000) that clearly identifies negative student images of mathematicians and mathematics.

When elementary school children are asked what they want to be when they grow up, the answer is seldom "I want to be a mathematician." While the reasons may be many, one seems to be that young children rarely know anyone who is a mathematician (Picker & Berry, 2000). Rarely are mathematicians portrayed on television or in the movies, and when they are, the picture is not flattering. Even the recent portrayal of John Nash as triumphant figure still depicts him as a schizophrenic triumphant hero. With no potent role models to counter stereotypes, the myth of mathematicians as antisocial misfits who can't dress themselves and spend their days only thinking about mathematics is perpetuated even by older students (Malkevitch, 1997). We both agreed that such representations of mathematics as an unattractive and unattainable profession underscore the need to help students construct more positive images.

The general public is not well versed in the history of mathematics or in the many careers available to students who major in mathematics. Elementary school teachers are no exception, having a limited conceptualization of the work of mathematicians (Cole, 1998; Hammond, 1978). Furinghetti (1993) found in her study that students believe mathematics is about skill drill and getting the right answer. If the mathematics being taught in their classrooms produced these notions, as Rock and Shaw suggest, then it is quite possible the teachers of these students will not assist their pupils in developing coherent structures around the nature of mathematics learning or help them to shape cultural norms about the career practices of mathematicians.

Having negative perceptions of mathematics as a learner therefore can make it difficult for students to imagine themselves in this career since their previous knowledge can impede future knowledge (NRC, 1999, p. 225). Having a teacher whose notion is one in which the work of a mathematician is limited to solving hard problems or writing math textbooks is troublesome for two reasons: first, this teacher is likely to teach mathematics in a rote, algorithmic fashion, having students work on problems to get right answers without discussion and collaboration; second, preconceived teacher assumptions such as this reduce the possibility that students will view mathematics as an exciting career choice and develop a range of mathematician images for their future career considerations. Thus, this situation continues to fulfill the predicted decline in students enrolling in advanced mathematics courses (Garfunkel & Young, 1998).

If students are taught mathematics with an emphasis on rote, dull, test-driven work there is an unmistakable message being delivered that only those with "special math powers" can succeed in a career in the field of mathematics (Picker & Berry, 2000). Further, teaching mathematics as nothing more than arithmetic in which the focus is on product and not process most likely will leave students believing that the discipline of mathematics is boring and lacking any connection to real life.

Schoenfeld (1987) and Henrion (1997) have written about how mathematics is taught in classrooms. Both studies report that the teaching of mathematics often centers on computation and the acquisition of a "right answer" with the prominent instructional style being lecture, teacher as authority, memorization of formulas, and practice in skills. If this is what our students experience as mathematics how can we expect more than a few to want to pursue a career in this area?

The two of us concluded that the mathematics that students encounter in classrooms should offer learning experiences that broaden both content and pedagogy beyond rules and formulaic procedures to include mathematics work that relates to student interests, families, and real-life circumstances and that provide students with opportunities to solve open-ended, challenging, messy problems. Students need to work in groups and exchange ideas in the process of seeking multiple reasonable answers to their own mathematical curiosities if we want them to perceive mathematics as a possible career choice. Maybe then we might see a trend toward students opting for careers in mathematics that they envision as exciting, challenging, attainable, and stimulating.

This research that began as collegial conversation helped Scott and me to better understand our roles in helping to stop this decline in students seeking careers in mathematics. We both altered our teaching in order to raise student awareness of the problem, and we worked with classroom teachers to provide real-life examples of mathematicians and their work.

WHAT DOES CRITICAL THINKING MEAN FOR LEARNING IN ALL CONTENT AREAS?

This book has presented strategies for infusing mathematics reasoning and critical thinking into the school day in spite of all the constraints and demands teachers and administrators face today. Critical thinking is not a skill needed only in math class. Being a critical thinker enhances learning in all content areas. Whether the problem being posed is in regards to social studies, literature, or science, the ability to look at the problem, to assess what is being asked, to examine a variety of solution pathways, to listen to seek other opinions and ideas, and to apply what is learned to new situations are what differentiate critical thinkers from those students who can only memorize and respond with textbook solutions. Students will be more apt to view their world from the perspective of possibilities than to see life as a series of obstacles without knowing how to find novel solutions. The sense of empowerment we provide students when we allow them to find their own solutions is a life skill that will linger long after the June graduation from high school.

When I team-taught fourth grade with Carol, we often wondered how our students fared when they left our classroom and became fifth graders in a variety of new instructional environments. Did our style of teaching help or hinder students when they found themselves in different classroom situations? Would they remain invested in the process of learning as much as in the product? Would they still question other students and engage in discussions about thinking? How much of what they were learning with us would transfer to new learning experiences? Was the role of teacher embedded in the process or would students manage to continue to develop a habit of reflective thinking without our direct direction? We received a partial answer to some of these questions one day when a fifth-grade teacher came to our room at the end of the day. "I wanted to talk with you two for a minute. What is it you do in your class that makes your students think they can solve *any* problem?" Carol and I looked at each other and smiled. "I'm serious," the teacher said. "No matter what problem is presented, I can always tell which students came from your classroom—they are the ones who are eager to solve the problems. It doesn't matter if it is a social studies question or a classroom management issue; your students are the ones who always take the lead in the discussions and the ones who have much to offer in terms of solutions to think about. They are always saying, well, what if …"

This teacher exchange gave Carol and me much to think about and was the beginning of many new questions for us to ponder. We wanted to do more

teacher research as we thought about the implications of inquiry-based learning for our teaching and learning beyond our classroom.

I have participated in multiple research and evaluation studies that have
looked at various aspects of teacher development. If I were asked to identify the
one teacher characteristic that identifies an exceptional teacher, it would be the
desire to know more. There is little energy and excitement in complacency. I'm
not talking about jumping on every educational bandwagon that is promoted
in a given year. I am suggesting, however, that teachers need to remain knowledge hungry and continuously seek new ways to make their teaching better.
Anthony's story below is an example of a teacher wanting to know more.

JOURNAL REFLECTING DURING PROBLEM
SOLVING VERSUS AFTER PROBLEM SOLVING

Sometimes I think the question "Why" could be the new symbol of education.

Anthony, a graduate student who was student teaching in a large urban fourth-
grade classroom, decided he wanted the students to experiment with using
math journals. His story is one of particular interest for this chapter as it illuminates not only Anthony's reflections on his teaching, but also his reflections
on his students' reflections.

> As I asked my students to explore while they engaged in mathematics, I did the
> same with how I taught math, and taught in general. Challenge my students to
> explore the unknown and to ask questions. So as they do, I took my own chal-
> lenge and asked myself, "Will integrating writing and math really work?" It was
> my job to prove it. Now I ask, "What took so long to do so?"

Anthony set about to read everything regarding the use of math journals in
the classroom. He read articles written by people who have used journal writing as part of their math instruction. From his readings he garnered a new sense
of what teachers believed worked and what they reported did not. He began to
shape a set of expectations for himself and his students. In his words:

> My goal was to become a better math teacher and to find ways to really recog-
> nize what my students understood in math. I had fantasies of us transforming
> into master mathematicians. Things don't always work out in the classroom as
> they do in our dreams.

Anthony's first journal writing assignment was for students to reflect on
their work in a math lesson involving subtracting large numbers. He developed prompts for the students to use: "What did you do in today's lesson?"
and "What did you learn?" After only a few minutes, students were proclaim-
ing they were finished. Astonished, and wondering how the students could

possibly be finished writing, Anthony walked around to check on the journal writing. What the students were writing didn't teach him anything about what they understood about subtracting large numbers. He walked about asking questions such as what cards? What was the digits game? What answers did you share? What did you learn? What strategy? Students responded in detail to his questions. He asked them, "Why didn't you write that?" These vague and unspecific journal entries left Anthony confused and frustrated. He had modeled writing a sample journal with the whole class and emphasized the importance of writing the journal entry as if the reader was not in class that day. Anthony began to wonder what he needed to do to get a different set of journal writings. For some reason the students were not putting their thought processes into words without prompts from him. He had to keep asking them what their answers meant, to tell the steps they used to solve the problem, what the answer means, or what they were still wondering about. Why couldn't students write this without intervention? What about the prompts needed to be changed?

> After talking to students throughout the week, what I began to realize was that they really had a lot of difficulty reflecting on what they did in math, in the sense that they are now writing about what they previously did in our lesson. What they are thinking about now is what they did, not what they are doing. When I talked with them during lessons their explanations were rich with understanding and those were the moments I needed to take advantage of for writing. By having the students do lessons and then later write about the experience, I was taking away that moment of "mathematical thinking." It's that thinking and understanding that I wanted to capture in the math journal. It became clear quickly that, for my students, writing had to become part of their problem solving.

Anthony began to understand that the students' difficulties writing and reflecting were in part due to the fact that they hadn't had experience with journal writing. His research validated this—a failure of journal writing to have a positive impact on problem solving.

> Expository writing, however, seems to engage students more in the process of problem solving by asking them to analyze a problem and explain a solution. So if posing a problem was what it was going to take for students to express those analytical skills and explanations, that's what the next journal would ask them to do. It specifically asked them to solve a division problem as part of their journal (including writing steps in solving) and we attached that same prompt to the end—what did you learn from today's lesson? The results were a welcomed improvement as students unleashed deep explanations of their problem-solving processes in writing. This is where I could truly find that student understanding I was searching for—in their actual work during a problem! Not only did these open windows for me to see what the students understood, it did the same for them. It allowed them to bring to life and see for themselves what they did and did not know, and consequently, when asked what they learned, it was a question of significantly less difficulty.

Anthony posed the following problem for students to write about in their journals: If you had to teach someone who has never done division before (doesn't even know what it is), how could you explain in words what it means to do division? Use 94 divided by 4 to help you. What do you do with remainders?

The following are two examples of student journal entries.

I would tell them that division is multiplication backward like 94 divided by 4. You have to find a multiplication factor that will give you 94 (4 x __ = 94). But sometimes you will get remainders. With remainders you will have to find a way to have a fair share. But when you have a remainder you will have to find something that you can cut equally.

Example:

I have 94 cookies and 4 friends with me.
  1   2   3   4
23   23   23   23
remainder: 2
Each one of my friends get 23 cookies but there are 2 cookies left. So I could cut them up in half and each one will get 23½ cookies.
Mathew

Division is multiplication backward. If you don't know what this means,
94 divided by 4 = ? Then you could look at the question a different way. $4 \times ? = 94$.
If you still have trouble you can use this strategy: $4 \times 20 = 80$; $4 \times 25 = 100$.
Then find what's between 20 and 25 to get to 94. 94 divided by 4 means how many groups of 4 can go into 94? If it can't what is the remainder?
With the remainder you don't always need to keep it for yourself. If you have food that is pretty big, you can always split it. If you don't have food, you have to have something else you can give away to someone (a friend, family member, or a homeless person who needs things).
Joy

Anthony concluded that his students were more able to write about their problem-solving strategies and learning as they were in the process of problem solving and learning and *not* as a journal exercise after the activity was completed. Students were explaining conceptual understandings and communicating thinking in process—thus clarifying thinking and justifying with examples.

TEACHER AS RESEARCHER THOUGHTS

Any good researcher knows that it is important to share with readers something of herself as the researcher. Throughout this volume in the Teacher as Researcher Thoughts sections, I have given ideas for research for you to consider. In this chapter, I want to share with you a little of myself as I explain, in brief, why I wrote this book.

CODA

Why? Why did I want to write this book? By now I am sure it is no surprise to you that my passion for mathematics education is like a snowball barreling down a winter hillside or the "1812 Overture" building in a crescendo to cannon fire. My fervor began slowly and is no longer stoppable. I am concerned that testing and curriculum demands limit critical thinking opportunities in classrooms all across the country and that teachers feel increasing pressures to drill their students to do well on tests and to "cover the curriculum." This book is about finding ways to help students become critical thinkers throughout the school day because we can no longer afford to think of critical thinking as a pedagogy of enrichment. Our world needs critical thinkers more than ever before.

We need citizens who ask "Why, Why is this so?" Why can't we as educators nurture a population of concerned people who think about their roles in finding solutions and altering outcomes in both personal and global situations? This calls for reasoning and questioning and not routine acceptance. Why is my credit card interest so high? Is that loan offer a good or bad choice? When a family is confronted with a medical decision with life-or-death consequences they need to engage in a critical review of options for treatment, outcome probabilities, and long-term quality of life implications. Why are the ice caps melting? Why are the tragic situations of genocide, famine, and disease allowed to continue in many parts of the world? Why does health care remain unobtainable for so many people in our world? Why are poverty rates increasing at what seems to be the speed of melting ice cream and why do our most needy children lack the educational resources that others enjoy?

When we teach children that problem solving is using a formula to find a "right" answer, we are, in the most optimistic of circumstances, perpetuating the global status quo of the world. In the worst-case scenario, we are stopping the development of valuable, precious minds that might create all sorts of solutions to reverse or alter many catastrophic endings. In a nutshell, we are relying on too few people to solve the many problems we face in our neighborhoods, our country, and our world. We must help our students to develop the tools to solve complex problems of humanity and to equip them with reflective habits that will enable them to see critically their role in creating solutions.

Imagine the gain for humanity if we all focused on enabling children to develop as critical thinkers rather than as robotic test takers. I will leave you with that thought to ponder and to conclude for yourself what that might mean in our world.

References

Aker, S., & Karlin, B. (1992). *What comes in 2's, 3's, and 4's?* New York: Simon & Schuster.

Aronson, D. (2006, September). The First Amendment: A powerful way to teach critical thinking. *The Council Chronicle.*

Artzt, A. F. (1996). Developing problem-solving behaviors by assessing communication in cooperative learning groups. In P. C. Elliott & M. J. Kenney (Eds.), *Communication in mathematics, K–12 and beyond* (pp. 116–125). Reston, VA: NCTM.

Baratta-Lorton, M. (1976). *Math Their Way.* Menlo Park, CA: Addison Wesley.

Bennett S., & Kalish, N. (2006). *The case against homework: How homework is hurting our children and what we can do about it.* New York: Random House.

Berenstain, S., & Berenstain, J. 1997. *The Berenstain bears and the homework hassle.* New York: Random House.

Bogart, A. (2001). *A director prepares: Seven essays on art in theatre.* New York: Routledge.

Brooks, J., & Brooks, M. (1999). *In search of understanding: The case for constructivist classrooms.* Alexandria, VA: Association for Supervision and Curriculum Development.

Bruner, J. (1986). *Actual minds, possible worlds.* Cambridge, MA: Harvard University Press.

Burns, M., & Silbey, R. (2001, April). Math journals boost real learning. *Instructor, 110*(7), 18–20.

Carpenter, T., Franke, M., & Levi, L. (2003). *Thinking mathematically: Integrating arithmetic and algebra in elementary school.* Portsmouth, NH: Heinemann.

Cazden, C. B. (2001). *Classroom discourse: The language of teaching and learning* (2nd ed.). Portsmouth, NH: Heinemann.

Cheng, K.-M. (2006, March). *The importance of arts education.* Presentation given at UNESCO's World Conference on Arts Education: Building Creative Capacities for the 21st Century, Lisbon, Portugal.

Ciardiello, A. (1998). Did you ask a good question today? *Journal of Adolescent & Adult Literacy, 42*(3).

Cobb, P. & Hodge, L. (2002). A relational perspective on issues of cultural diversity and equity as they play out in the mathematics classroom. *Mathematical Thinking and Learning, 4* (2–3), 249–284.

Coerr, E. (1999). *Sadako and the thousand paper cranes.* New York: Puffin.

Cohen, M. (2006). *First grade takes a test.* Long Island City, NY: Star Bright Books.

Cole, K. C. (1998, July 14). Math whizzes want respect in equation. *The Los Angeles Times.*

Coville, B. (1993). *Aliens ate my homework.* New York: Pocket Books.

Crist, James. (2004). *What to do when you're scared and worried: A guide for kids.* Minneapolis, MN: Free Spirit Publishing.

Dewey, J. (1929/1960). *The quest for certainty.* New York: Capricorn.

Dewey, J. (1933/1998). *How we think.* New York: Houghton Mifflin.

Dewey, J. (1938/1963). *Experience and education.* New York: Collier.

Donaldson, M. (1978). *Children's minds.* Glasgow: William Collins Sons.

Duckworth, E. (1987). *"The having of wonderful ideas" and other essays on teaching and learning.* New York: Teachers College Press.

Dweck, C. (2000). *Self-theories: Their role in motivation, personality, and development.* Philadelphia: Taylor & Francis.

Edwards, P. (2005). *Researcher uses parent stories to help teachers understand students and their families* [Educational Briefings]. East Lansing, MI: College of Education, Michigan State University.

Eisner, E. (2003, May). Questionable assumptions about schooling. *Phi Delta Kappan, 84*(9), 648–657.

Ennis, C., & Cauley, M. (2002). Creating urban classroom communities worthy of trust. *Journal of Curriculum Studies, 34*(2), 149–172.

Epstein, J. L. (2006). Prospects for change: Preparing educators for school, family, and community partnerships. *Peabody Journal of Education, 81*(2), 81.

Finchler, J. (2003). *Testing Miss Malarkey.* New York: Walker Books for Young Readers

Fingerman, B. (2006). *Recess pieces.* Milwaukie, OR: Dark Horse.

Flournoy, V. (1985). *The patchwork quilt.* New York: Penguin Books.

Fosnot, C. (Ed.). (1996). *Constructivism: Theory, perspectives, and practice.* New York: Teachers College Press.

Freire, P. (1970). *Pedagogy of the oppressed.* New York: Herder and Herder.

Freire, P. (1973). *Education for critical consciousness.* New York: Seabury Press.

Freire, P. (1996). *Pedagogy of hope.* New York: Continuum.

Furinghetti, F. (1993). Images of mathematics outside the community of mathematicians: Evidence and explanations. *For the Learning of Mathematics, 13*(2), 33–38.

Garfunkel, S. A., & Young, G. S. (1998). The sky is falling, *Notices of the AMS, 45*(2), 256–257.

Greenes, C., & Schulman, L. (1996). Communication processes in mathematical explorations and investigations. In P. C. Elliott & M. J. Kenny (Eds.), *Communication in mathematics, K–12 and beyond* (pp. 159–169). Reston, VA: NCTM.

Hammond, A. L. (1978). Mathematics, our invisible culture. In L. A. Steen (Ed.), *Mathematics today: Twelve informal essays* (pp. 16–25). New York: Springer-Verlag.

Henrion, C. (1997). *Women in mathematics: The addition of difference.* Bloomington: Indiana University Press.

Heron, A. (2003). A study of agency: Multiple constructions of choice and decision making in an inquiry-based summer school program for struggling readers. *Journal of Adolescent & Adult Literacy, 46*(7), 568–579.

Hickam, H. (1999). *October sky: A memoir.* New York: Dell.

Holbrook, S. (1997). *The dog ate my homework: Poems.* Honesdale, PA: Boyds Mills Press.

Huhn, C. (2005). How many points is this worth? *Educational Leadership, 63*(3), 81–82.

Kohn, A. (2006). *The homework myth: Why our kids get too much of a bad thing.* Cambridge, MA: Da Capo Press.

Kozol, J. (1991). *Savage inequalities: Children in America's schools.* New York: HarperCollins.

Kozol, J. (2000, May). An unequal education. *School Library Journal, 46*(5), 46–49.

Kravolec, E., & Buell, J. (2000). *The end of homework: How homework disrupts families, overburdens children, and limits learning.* Boston: Beacon Press.

Lambert, M. (1990). When the problem is not a question and the solution is not an answer: Mathematical knowing and teaching. *American Educational Research Journal, 27,* 29–63.

Levy, S. (1996). *Starting from scratch: One classroom builds its own curriculum.* Portsmouth, NH: Heinemann.

Livingstone, I., & Izard, J. (Eds.). (1993). *Best of SET mathematics* [SET: Research Information for Teachers, special issue]. Camberwell, Victoria, Australia: Australian Council for Education Research.

Malkevitch, J. (1997). Discrete mathematics and public perceptions of mathematics. In J. G. Rosenstein, D. S. Franzblau, & F. S. Roberts (Eds.), *Discrete mathematics in the schools* (pp. 89–97). Providence, RI: American Mathematical Society/NCTM.

McVarish, J. (1994). *A formula for mathematics reform?* Unpublished master's thesis, Lesley College, Cambridge, MA.

McVarish, J., & Solloway, S. S. (2002). Self-evaluation: Creating a classroom without unhealthy competitiveness. *The Educational Forum, 66*(3), 253–260.

Mezirow, J. (1990). Conclusion: Toward transformative learning and emancipatory education. In J. Mezirow and Associates (Eds.), *Fostering critical reflection in adulthood: A guide to transformative and emancipatory education.* San Francisco: Jossey-Bass.

Mezirow, J. (1998). On critical reflection. *Adult Education Quarterly, 48*(3), 185–98.

National Council of Teachers of Mathematics. (1989). *Curriculum and evaluation standards for school mathematics.* Reston, VA: Author.

National Council of Teachers of Mathematics. (2000). *Principles and standards for school mathematics: An overview.* Reston, VA: Author.

National Research Council. (1989). *Everybody counts: A report to the nation on the future of mathematics education.* Washington, DC: National Academy Press.

National Research Council. (1999). *How people learn.* Washington, DC: National Academy Press.

National Research Council. (2001). *Adding it up: Helping children learn mathematics.* Washington, DC: National Academy Press.

National Research Council, Mathematical Sciences Education Board. (1990). *Reshaping school mathematics.* Washington, DC: National Academy Press.

National Science Board. (2004). *An emerging and critical problem of the science and engineering labor force: A companion to science and engineering indicators 2004.* Arlington, VA: National Science Foundation.

National Science Board. (2004). *Science and engineering indicators 2004.* Arlington, VA: National Science Foundation.

O'Brien, T. C., & Wallach, C. (2006). From the classroom: A lesson on logical necessity. *Teaching Children Mathematics, 13*(1), 46.

O'Neill, A. (2002). *The recess queen.* New York: Scholastic Press.

O'Neill, D. K., & Polman, J. L. (2004). Why educate "little scientists"? Examining the potential of practice-based scientific literacy. *Journal of Research in Science Teaching, 41,* 234–266.

Pappas, T. (1991). *Math talk: Mathematical ideas in poems for two voices.* San Carlos, CA: Wide World Publishing.

Paul, A. W. (1999). *Eight hands round: A patchwork alphabet.* New York: HarperCollins.

Pellegrini, A., & Bohn, C. (2005). The role of recess in children's cognitive performance and school adjustment. *Educational Researcher, 34*(1), 13–19.

Perkins, D. (1992). *Smart schools.* New York: Free Press.

Picker, S. H., & Berry, J. (2000). Investigating pupils' images of mathematicians. *Educational Studies in Mathematics, 43,* 65–94.

Resnick, L. B. (1987). Learning in school and out. *Educational Researcher, 16,* 13–20.

Robinson, K. (2001). *Out of our own minds: Learning to be creative.* Chichester, UK: Capstone.

Robinson, K. (2006, March). *Back to basics: Arts education in the 21st century.* Keynote address of UNESCO's World Conference on Arts Education: Building Creative Capacities for the 21st Century, Lisbon, Portugal.

Rock, D., & Shaw, J. M. (2000). Exploring children's thinking about mathematicians and their work. *Teaching Children Mathematics, 6*(9), 550–555.

Romain, T. (1997). *How to do homework without throwing up.* Minneapolis, MN: Free Spirit Publishing.

Rosenshine, B., Meister, C., & Chapman, S. (1996). Teaching students to generate questions: A review of the intervention studies. *Review of Educational Research, 66,* 181–221.

Rowan, T., & Bourne, B. (1994). *Thinking like mathematicians.* Portsmouth, NH: Heinemann.

Saljo, R. (1988, November). A week has seven days. Or does it? On bridging linguistic openness and mathematical precision. *For the Learning of Mathematics—An International Journal of Mathematics Education, 8*(3), 16–19.

Sarason, S. (2004). *And what do YOU mean by learning?* Portsmouth, NH: Heinemann.

Schoenfeld, A. H. (1987). What's all the fuss about metacognition? In A. H. Schoenfeld (Ed.), *Cognitive science and mathematics education* (pp. 189–215). Hillsdale, NJ: Lawrence Erlbaum.

Schön, D. (1983). *The reflective practitioner: How professionals think in action.* New York: Basic Books.

Schön, D. (1991). *The reflective turn: Case studies in and on educational practice.* New York: Teachers College Press.

Schumm, J. (2005). *How to help your child with homework: The complete guide to encouraging good study habits and ending the homework wars.* Minneapolis, MN: Free Spirit.

Scieszka, J., & Smith, L. (1995). *Math curse.* New York: Viking Juvenile.

Seuss, Dr., Prelutsky, J., & Smith, L. (1998). *Hooray for Diffendoofer day!* New York: Alfred A. Knopf.

Spielberg, Ellie. (2006). *Teamwork: Annual parent conference helps strengthen home-school partnerships.* New York Teacher: VXLVIII, n 7. United Federation of Teachers.

Stigler, J., & Hiebert, J. (1999). *The teaching gap: Best ideas from the world's teachers for improving education in the classroom.* New York: Free Press.

Tanner, M. L., & Casados, L. (1998). Promoting and studying discussions in math classes. *Journal of Adolescent and Adult Literacy, 41*(5), 342–351.

Trueba, H. (1989). *Raising silent voices: Educating linguistic minorities for the 21st century.* New York: Harper and Row.

Van De Walle, J. (2006). *Elementary and middle school mathematics: Teaching developmentally* (6th ed.) New York: Addison Wesley, Longman.

Vygotsky, L. S. (1978). *Mind in society: The development of higher psychological processes.* Cambridge, MA: Harvard University Press.

Vygotsky, L. S. (1962). *Language and thought.* Cambridge, MA: MIT Press.

Wayne, M. (2002). Getting smarter. In D. Worsley (Ed.), *Teaching for depth: Where math meets the humanities* (pp. 124–134). Portsmouth, NH: Heinemann.

Wells, G. (1993). Reevaluating the IRF sequence. A proposal for the articulation of theories of activity and discourse for the analysis of teaching and learning in the classroom. *Linguistics and Education, 5,* 1–37.

White, R. T., & Gunstone, R. F. (1992). *Probing understanding.* London: Falmer Press.

Wood, D., Bruner, J., & Ross, G. (1976). The role of tutoring in problem solving. *Journal of Child Psychology and Psychiatry, 17,* 89–100.

Yackel, E., & Cobb, P. (1996). Sociomathematical norms, argumentation, and autonomy in mathematics. *Journal for Research in Mathematics Education, 27,* 458–477.

Young, E. (1992). *Seven blind mice.* New York: Putnam Juvenile.

Index